T0023487

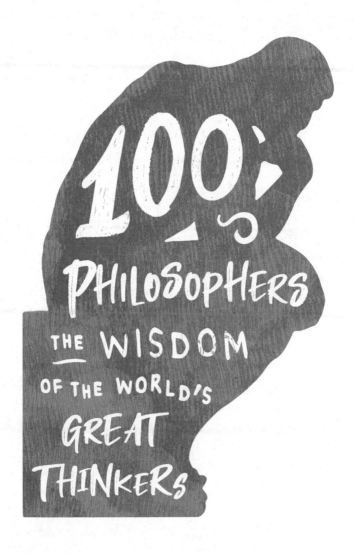

100 PHILOSOPHERS

THE WISDOM OF THE WORLD'S GREAT THINKERS

LESLEY LEVENE

Michael O'Mara Books Limited

First published in Great Britain in 2021 by
Michael O'Mara Books Limited
9 Lion Yard
Tremadoc Road
London SW4 7NQ

Copyright © Michael O'Mara Books Limited 2021

All rights reserved. You may not copy, store, distribute, transmit, reproduce or
otherwise make available this publication (or any part of it) in any form, or by
any means (electronic, digital, optical, mechanical, photocopying, recording
or otherwise), without the prior written permission of the publisher. Any
person who does any unauthorized act in relation to this publication may be
liable to criminal prosecution and civil claims for damages.

A CIP catalogue record for this book is available from the British Library.

Papers used by Michael O'Mara Books Limited are natural, recyclable
products made from wood grown in sustainable forests. The manufacturing
processes conform to the environmental regulations of the country of origin.

ISBN: 978-1-78929-370-8 in hardback print format
ISBN: 978-1-78929-371-5 in ebook format

1 2 3 4 5 6 7 8 9 10

Designed and typeset by Natasha Le Coultre
Printed and bound in UK by Bell & Bain Ltd, Glasgow

www.mombooks.com

MIX
Paper from
responsible sources
FSC® C007785

Introduction

For as long humans have been around, we have been wondering about how to make sense of our existence in the physical world and our place in the metaphysical greater scheme of things. Think of those early cave paintings ... With the power to reason comes the ability to question the nature and purpose of our lives. And that's where philosophy enters the picture.

In a book of quotes by great philosophers are the quotes or the philosophers themselves supposed to be more important? As in all things philosophical, that question is meant to start a conversation rather than to suggest that there's any right or wrong answer.

When looking for interesting quotes – ones that could actually be sourced as opposed to those that just popped up online as motivational thoughts for the day – the ideal was something pithy and instantly memorable that would encapsulate a particular philosopher's line of reasoning: René Descartes' 'I think therefore I am' stands out as the obvious example. The other ninety-nine quotes here might not quite hit the same 'sound bite' heights, but they all have something meaningful to say about the problems each particular philosopher was wrestling with at the time, and in some cases they have divorced themselves from their original context, working their way into common parlance: phrases like 'the banality of evil' and 'the ghost in the machine', for example. The quotes have been drawn from as wide a geographical area as possible and cover over two and a half thousand years of history, so they provide plenty of range and depth.

Because the philosophers are presented here chronologically, their quotes show interesting themes and trends becoming apparent in different areas as one thinker or group of thinkers is influenced by another and all are influenced by the events that are affecting their daily lives. The quotes themselves capture a particular moment in time, or the time of mind for that particular philosopher, and it would be foolish to imagine that great thinkers do not go on to adjust their opinions when circumstances demand it. The accompanying biographical information provides context for each quote and there is a wealth of further material out there, in books and online, for anyone who wants to explore further.

Whether you start from an interest in the Eastern philosophical tradition, with its roots in early China, or the Western philosophical tradition, which goes back to ancient Greece, reading this book will make you realize that there are similarities between the two. And when Western Europeans lost their links with the classical world after the end of the Roman Empire, it was Islamic philosophers who eventually reconnected them, adding their own ideas to their translations of the Greek classics. As time went on and philosophy looked beyond the academies and into the outside world, it broadened its scope to engage with fields as diverse as science and religion, history and politics, the law, the economy and human rights. Ideas come to the fore, have their moment and sink back again, but advances are made each time, so the sinking back is never as far.

That said, the one thing that struck me as I was compiling this book is that all the female philosophers included here have felt the need to continue to question the inferior role of women in society. I am a woman, so that jumped out at me. What about you? Who do you feel is speaking for you when you read through the quotes here?

Laozi

(6th century BCE)

'**A journey of a thousand miles begins with a single step.**'

Daodejing, 64

The Chinese philosopher Laozi (literally 'Old Master') is something of an enigma. Little is known of his life – if indeed he existed – but he is considered to be the man who inspired Daoism and its foundational text, the *Daodejing* ('Classic of the Way and Virtue'), which was compiled some 300 years after his putative death.

According to Sima Qian's monumental history of China, the *Shiji*, which was written in the late second and early first centuries BCE, Laozi was keeper of the archives at the Zhou court and it was there that he was visited by Confucius, who wanted to consult him on ritual matters. This has led some scholars to suggest that Laozi was an older contemporary of Confucius. 'Laozi cultivated Dao and virtue,' Sima Qian says, and 'his learning was devoted to self-effacement and not having fame'. Whether or not you take this at face value, the influence of Daoism is undeniable and Laozi is revered as its founder.

Both a philosophy and a religion, Daoism does not present a set of doctrines, but rather focuses on the importance of living in harmony with the Dao ('the Way'). The need is for balance at all times. There is a rhythmic flow between the natural world and human beings that remains in a state of flux, as all things are on a journey through life. To be part of the flow you need to embrace the principles of *ziran* (naturalness) and *wuwei* (non-action). Think too hard or try to put ideas into words and you will lose your way.

Born on the Greek island of Samos, Pythagoras visited centres of learning in Egypt and Babylonia before, around 530 BCE, establishing his own community in Croton, southern Italy. Adherents lived communally, with men and women treated equally and property held in common. Following a path of moral asceticism and ritual purification of the body rather than seeking worldly gain, he and his disciples believed in the transmigration of souls and the interconnectedness of all living things. However, no teachings were written down in Pythagoras's lifetime and after his death he became the stuff of legend.

Today Pythagoras is known primarily as a mathematician, thanks to the theorem named after him. According to later accounts, he held that the cosmos was structured according to moral principles and significant numerical relationships. Having worked out that mathematical ratios underpinned musical harmony, he concluded that mathematics, because of its power to purify, was fundamental to everything, with geometry its highest form. The imperfect physical world could be understood through the rigour imposed upon it by mathematical formulae – and not only the physical world but heavenly bodies too, through the 'music of the spheres'.

It is hard to separate Pythagoras's original thoughts from all the later mysticism, but his emphasis on a form of pure reality underlying surface appearances clearly influenced Plato, as well as other philosophers.

Pythagoras

(c.570–c.490 BCE)

'Number is the ruler
of forms and ideas.'

Iamblichus of Chalcis,
On the Pythagorean Life
(2nd century CE)

Confucius

(551–479 BCE)

'**Do not do to others
what you do not want
them to do to you.**'

The Analects, 15.23

Confucius was born into a noble clan, but his father died early, leaving the family with a place in society but little upon which to live. The young Confucius developed a reputation for being well versed in classical ritual and religious practices. When old enough, he travelled to his father's birthplace, Lu (in present-day Shandong Province), where he started to work for different aristocratic families and, over the years, took on a number of official roles.

Confucius's success led to rivals engineering his downfall and in 497 BCE he left Lu. For the next twelve years he went from court to court, in search of a benevolent ruler prepared to follow his guidance, and along the way he acquired a body of disciples. Returning to Lu, he then spent his final years teaching. After his death those disciples compiled *The Analects* as a record of their master's beliefs.

The picture that emerges shows Confucius as a great moral teacher who advocated a system of ritual practice that demonstrated how ideal social forms could regulate individual behaviour; developed a system of ethics grounded in a clear set of personal virtues; and formulated an approach to politics and society based on the family and the state. *The Analects* emphasizes the importance of a wide range of characteristics, including benevolence, righteousness, wisdom and trustworthiness, but when asked to name just one, Confucius went for reciprocity – which explains the quote here, another version of the 'golden rule' that continues to feature across cultures and over time.

Protagoras

(c.490–c.420 BCE)

'Man is the measure of all things.'

Quoted in Plato, *Theaetetus*

Protagoras was born in Abdera, an important Greek settlement on the coast of Thrace, but was a frequent visitor to Athens. It was there that he became one of the best-known sophists – scholars who would, for a fee, teach those wishing to make a name for themselves in public life the art of rhetoric.

His assertion that 'Man is the measure of all things' is the earliest expression of relativism – the belief that there are no external, objective standards and instead individuals must judge for themselves what they are seeing and feeling. While this might seem fairly uncontroversial in some areas – only you know whether you find the meal we're sharing delicious, for example – if you start applying the same logic to justice, virtue or truth someone could get hurt. Despite this, as far as Protagoras was concerned, nothing was inherently good or bad – and, what's more, it was pointless relying on the gods to determine right and wrong because there was no proof that they even existed.

It is but a short step from sophist to sophistry, with all its modern negative connotations, and although Protagoras was reputedly honest and well intentioned, his ideas were open to abuse by those wishing to make a bad case seem good. For this reason his ideas were later challenged by Socrates in Plato's *Protagoras*, one of the Socratic dialogues, and pilloried by the comic playwright Aristophanes in *The Birds*. However, no one can deny that Protagoras got the relativism and agnosticism balls rolling.

He left behind no books, he established no school of philosophy, and yet Socrates is widely seen as the founding father of Western philosophy. This is because he was the first to turn philosophy away from speculation about the origins of the universe and towards a study of the ethics and moral precepts underpinning human behaviour.

Most of our information about Socrates' opinions – or rather, his way of reaching opinions – comes from Plato, a fellow Athenian philosophical heavyweight who was one of his disciples. In Plato's books we are presented with dialogues between Socrates and a range of different people with a view to exploring beliefs about such fundamental concepts as justice, courage, moderation, wisdom and piety – which Socrates refers to as 'virtues'. According to Plato, Socrates claimed to know nothing himself; but that was never the aim. Instead he wanted to challenge people to defend their ideas on the basis of logic. His role was to expose the contradictions and flaws in their arguments. Then, once false logic had been stripped away, people would be in a position to come up with universally applicable definitions of the virtues that would lay the foundations for the deepest moral good.

Righteous living was the key, but his endless challenging of popular beliefs set Socrates on a collision course with the Athenian state. Tried and found guilty of introducing new gods and corrupting the youth, he chose to drink hemlock and died.

Socrates

(c.470–399 BCE)

'The unexamined life is not worth living.'

Quoted in Plato, *Apology*

Plato

(c. 427–347 BCE)

'Wonder is the
feeling of a philosopher,
and philosophy
begins in wonder.'

Theaetetus

Born in Athens into an influential family, Plato might have pursued a political career, but once he became a student of Socrates everything changed. Understandably upset by his teacher's trial and death, Plato left Athens for over a decade. On his return he established the Academy, where philosophical, mathematical and scientific ideas were studied to help find ways of living a balanced life and establishing a just state.

Most of Plato's works are dialogues in which Socrates aims to tease out the truth at the heart of any discussion by cross-examining different interlocutors. With this rigorous, challenging method of inquiry, Plato provided a framework that has influenced Western philosophy ever since.

He believed that earthly objects are just pale imitations of their changeless perfect versions, called 'forms' or 'ideas'. Humans are like prisoners chained in a cave, seeing the world only through shadows cast on the wall. The philosopher's role is to lead those able to understand out into the light of true knowledge. As with earthly objects and perfect forms, so with the body and the immortal soul, which can exist independently. The soul consists of three parts: one that satisfies basic desires, one that responds to active qualities and one that represents intellect. A wise mind keeps all three in balance. And the parts correspond to social classes: rulers, soldiers and common people. For a harmonious, just society each class must know its place, with philosophers advising rulers to help them fulfil their role.

Diogenes

(c.400–323 BCE)

'I am looking for a man.'

Diogenes Laertius,

Lives of Eminent Philosophers

(3rd century CE)

Having been exiled from his hometown of Sinope (now in Turkey), Diogenes headed for Athens, where he became a student of the philosopher Antisthenes, who had himself studied with Socrates. Together, Antisthenes and Diogenes founded the school of philosophical thought known as Cynicism.

Although there are no contemporary records, we have endless stories about Diogenes's ostentatious disregard for creature comforts, not to mention social niceties. He is said to have lived in a tub 'like a dog' (*kunikos* in ancient Greek, hence Cynic) and to have had no qualms about urinating in public. On hearing Plato's definition of man as a featherless biped, he presented the eminent philosopher with a plucked chicken. As for the quote here, Diogenes reputedly walked around Athens in broad daylight carrying a lantern; when asked why, he claimed to be looking for an honest man.

Beneath these eccentricities lie the basic tenets of Cynicism, with its emphasis on self-sufficiency and asceticism in order to attain the mental clarity needed to live a natural life and flourish. Diogenes felt that people had been lured into living badly, influenced by the dictates of civilization, and should instead go back to basics, eating when hungry, sleeping when tired and generally ignoring conventions. Over time, the nuance disappeared, leaving the modern definition of a cynic as someone who sees other people as being motivated purely by self-interest.

Aristotle

(384–322 BCE)

' All men by nature desire to know. '

Metaphysics

Born in Stagira, Macedonia, Aristotle went at the age of seventeen to Plato's Academy in Athens. He spent some twenty years there, first as a student and then as a teacher.

His extant works started life as lecture notes on a wide range of subjects, including logic, metaphysics, ethics, political science, rhetoric and poetry, not to mention marine biology. As well as acquiring detailed knowledge in specific fields, Aristotle developed a generally applicable system of logical reasoning, drawing conclusions from premises assumed to be true: so, 'All men are mortal; Socrates is a man; therefore Socrates is mortal.' As for metaphysics and the very fundamentals of existence, he concluded that all things have 'substance', comprising both matter and form – a step on from Plato, who saw the two as separate, and an approach that worked for medieval religious thinkers. Regarding ethics, the only way to achieve happiness is through moderation – at the 'golden mean', between the extremes of surfeit and lack. Ethics led seamlessly on to politics, which was a question of how to ensure the individual's happiness within wider society, finding that elusive middle path.

Mencius

(371–289 BCE)

‘ **When in one's conduct one
vigorously exercises altruism, humanity
is not far to seek, but right by.** ’

The Book of Mencius, 7A.4

Like Confucius, Mencius was born in Shandong Province, and
some sources claim that he even studied with Confucius's
grandson. He is certainly referred to as the 'Second Sage' of
Confucianism. He lived during the Warring States period (475–
221 BCE), when rival rulers slogged it out for control of China.

For many years Mencius travelled the country, searching
for a ruler who would adopt Confucian moral and political
practices. He based his ethical system on the belief that
people were born good and would remain so if given the
right conditions in which to flourish. Once rulers provided
security, moral growth would follow. Like Confucius, Mencius
emphasized the importance of generosity of spirit, a sense
of duty, politeness and a love of learning. He also offered
practical advice on everything from foreign policy to taxation
and public building projects. Sadly, he never found his ideal
ruler, but his conversations with candidates along the way,
and with his disciples, were recorded after his death in *The
Book of Mencius* – one of the 'Four Books' of Confucianism.

Zhuangzi

(c. 370–286 BCE)

'Once Zhuang Zhou dreamed he was a butterfly, a butterfly flitting and fluttering around, happy with himself and doing as he pleased. He didn't know he was Zhuang Zhou. Suddenly he woke up, and there he was, solid and unmistakable Zhuang Zhou. But he didn't know if he were Zhuang Zhou who had dreamed he was a butterfly or a butterfly dreaming he was Zhuang Zhou. Between Zhuang Zhou and a butterfly, there must be *some* distinction! This is called the Transformation of Things.'

Zhuangzi

Nothing is known about his life from contemporary sources, but Zhuangzi (whose name also appears as Zhuang Zhou) is credited with writing some if not all of the *Zhuangzi*, which, together with the *Daodejing*, provides the textual and philosophical basis of Daoist thought.

Daoism focuses on the place of the individual in nature rather than in society, with each person looking to adapt to the rhythms of the natural world and so follow the Dao or Way. Zhuangzi taught that whatever can be known or said *of* the Dao can never *be* the Dao, because the Dao has no beginning and no end. Life is the continuous transformation of the infinite and all-encompassing Dao, in which events take their course and one situation cannot be valued more highly than another.

Zhuangzi's relativism finds expression in his famous butterfly dream, in which there is no omniscient, independent voice to judge between opposing perspectives. This realization should encourage people to attach less importance to social conventions, and to such binaries as right and wrong, self and others, and life and death. Without wasting emotional energy on concerns of this sort, with no preconceived goals or ideas of what is correct, a more spontaneous response becomes possible. And that holds for butterflies as well as for human beings.

Born on Samos to Athenian parents, Epicurus taught in Asia Minor before setting up his own school, the Garden – so called for obvious reasons – in Athens. A sign at the entrance apparently read: 'Stranger, here you will do well to tarry; here our highest good is pleasure.'

Epicurus held that the ultimate goal for human beings was happiness, by which he meant absence of physical pain and mental unrest. He identified fear of death and subsequent punishment as the main causes of anxiety, with that anxiety then prompting irrational and extreme desires to fend off the evil day. A committed empiricist, he was sure that direct observation and deduction were the only things needed to explain the world, leaving no room for transcendent beings who controlled human lives or for souls that survived after death. Once fears and unreasonable desires were eliminated, he felt sure that people would be free to pursue more modest and achievable pleasures and so enjoy the peace of mind that followed.

For Epicurus friendship was one of the greatest pleasures in life and 'natural' desires, such as food and shelter, were more worthwhile than 'vain' desires, such as wealth and power, being achievable goals that offered everyone a practical way of flourishing in the here and now.

Epicurus

(341–270 BCE)

'Death, the most awful of
evils, is nothing to us, seeing
that when we are, death
is not come, and when
death is come, we are not.'

Diogenes Laertius,
Lives of Eminent Philosophers
(3rd century CE)

Zou Yan

(c.305–240 BCE)

'First he had to examine small objects, and from these he drew conclusions about large ones, until he reached what was without limit.'

Sima Qian, *Shiji*
(late 2nd–early 1st century BCE)

Zou Yan was another Chinese philosopher from Shandong Province who came to the fore during the unsettled Warring States period (474–221 BCE). An important member of the 'naturalist' or Yin-Yang school of thinkers, who concerned themselves with metaphysics and the natural sciences, he was interested in the workings that underpinned the relationship between the human world and the cosmos.

Yin and yang were two naturally harmonious complementary forces that controlled the ebb and flow of the cosmos. Yin was associated with the human world, and female qualities: softness, darkness, submissiveness, cold; while yang was associated with the heavens and a set of corresponding male qualities: hardness, light, forcefulness, heat. The cosmos as a whole was an essential enduring unity but was never static; rather, it was a dynamic interaction of yin and yang, their qualities in constant flux – winter leading to summer, night to day and so on.

Zou Yan combined yin and yang with another set of forces, known as the 'Five Powers' – wood, fire, earth, metal and water – which had their own qualities. On a cosmological level, they too played into the constant dynamic that determined the rhythms of life. So, wood was paramount in spring, but as summer approached the power of fire grew, followed in midsummer by earth, in autumn by metal and in winter by water. Not only the natural world, but also various aspects of human behaviour – such as the rise and fall of dynasties – could be explained by the influence of such forces, the whole cosmos being rooted in this system of correlations.

Seneca

(c.4 BCE–65 CE)

' **Fire is the test of gold;
adversity, of strong men.** '

'On Providence', *Moral Essays*

It was during his banishment in Corsica that the Stoic
Lucius Annaeus Seneca wrote moral essays on topics such
as providence, steadfastness, the happy life, virtue, anger,
tranquillity and forgiveness, and well over a hundred letters
discussing ethical issues, all of which he related to his own
personal experiences. Throughout, he emphasized self-
control, certain that no one can be considered great until
they have learned to master themselves and their desires.
Setbacks should be treated as tests that will strengthen us,
while strong emotions are traps to enslave us.

He was recalled to Rome to tutor the young Nero and
then, when Nero became emperor in 54 CE, he assumed the
role of adviser. For some years all went well, but it proved
impossible to retain the unstable emperor's confidence and,
although Seneca retired from public life in 62 CE, three years
later Nero ordered him to commit suicide. Following his
Stoic principles this time, Seneca calmly slit his veins, took
poison and, just to make sure, jumped into a scalding bath.

Marcus Aurelius

(121–80 CE)

'**Nothing happens to anybody which he is not fitted by nature to bear.**'

Meditations, V.18

The Roman emperor Marcus Aurelius, the last great Stoic philosopher, lived through one of the worst plagues in European history, which is thought to have claimed the lives of around five million people, possibly even his own. At the same time, there was unrest in the northern and eastern parts of the empire, which meant that the emperor had military problems to contend with too.

It was against this tense background that he wrote his *Meditations*, drawing on Stoic ideas to come up with ways of dealing with the physical and mental fallout of illness, anxiety and loss. Marcus Aurelius stressed the importance of distinguishing between things that can't be controlled, by which he meant events, and things that can, by which he meant our responses to those events. For him, the way we respond is up to us, and once we learn – through wisdom, patience and self-discipline – how to weather the storm, there's nothing we can't handle.

St Augustine of Hippo

(354–430 CE)

'Give me chastity and continence – but not yet!'

Confessions

Born in North Africa to a Christian mother and a pagan father, Augustine brought his early skills in classical philosophy to bear on his growing interest in Christian doctrine to become one of the most influential thinkers in the Western Church.

He flirted with different philosophical approaches in his quest for the true path, working his way through Manichaeism, which saw the world as a constant struggle between good and evil, and scepticism, which focused on seeing both sides of an argument to avoid becoming dogmatic in outlook, before seeming to settle on Neoplatonism, which attempted to account for the obvious discrepancies between a flawed world and a perfect, and perfectible, mind. From there it was but a short step to God: Augustine converted to Christianity in 387, was ordained a priest in 391 and became Bishop of Hippo, in Algeria, in 396.

His *Confessions* is both a spiritual autobiography and an original work of philosophy, with interesting ideas on the nature of time (it's all in the mind). In his later book *The City of God*, he compares the heavenly kingdom with the City of Men, the former eternal and accessible by the intellect, the latter transient and always at risk from baser human instincts. The two coexist on earth, with the Church representing the City of God, offering salvation to those who follow the rules. And those rules include avoiding lust — hence the well-known quote from Augustine's autobiography.

Boethius

(c.480–524 CE)

'Nothing is miserable
but what is thought so,
and contrariwise, every
estate is happy if he that
bears it be content.'

The Consolation of Philosophy

The Roman philosopher and statesman Anicius Manlius Severinus Boethius links the philosophers of ancient Greece and the theologians of medieval Europe.

A member of the Senate in Rome, he was appointed consul in 510 and then chief minister to Theodoric, king of the Ostrogoths and ruler of Italy. However, in 523 he fell from favour, accused of treason, and after a year in prison in Pavia he was killed. It was during his imprisonment that he wrote *The Consolation of Philosophy*, a dialogue between the personification of Philosophy and the author, who has been made distraught by his change in fortune and the unfairness of a world where the wicked prosper at the expense of the good. As their discussions progress, Philosophy explains that it's all a matter of perspective. Earthly fortune is transient and true happiness can never be achieved by chasing power or pleasure. Only by embracing virtue, which remains constant, and by acting well can one attain the perfect good – or God.

For a millennium *The Consolation* was up there with the Bible as one of the most widely read books, its author the pre-eminent philosophical and theological writer in the Latin-speaking world.

Avicenna – from the Arabic Ibn Sina – was both a great philosopher and a great doctor. Indeed, he saw philosophy as the cure for ignorance, entitling one of his major works *The Book of Healing*. Born in modern-day Uzbekistan near Bukhara, an important centre of culture and commerce on the Silk Road, he had access to well-stocked libraries, notably texts by Aristotle.

Avicenna took elements from Aristotle and also later classical thinkers, blending them with Islam, in both its theological and its mystical aspects, to form a coherent system that covered every area of life. He saw the various strands of philosophical knowledge as a unified whole that should be added to constantly, and was interested in people's ability to acquire such knowledge rationally, suggesting the primacy of the soul in this regard. A devout Muslim, he identified what he called the 'necessary existent' – an overarching entity that cannot *not* exist and is essential to everything else. And the necessary existent is God, without whom there would be no flame in the glass lamp.

Whether or not people agreed with him, Avicenna set the intellectual agenda in the East, his views fundamental to later developments in philosophy, science and religion. From the twelfth century, Latin translations of his philosophy appeared in the West, influencing medieval and Renaissance scholars, while his *Canon of Medicine* was used in European medical schools until the seventeenth century.

Avicenna

(980–1037)

'The soul is like a
glass lamp, and knowledge
is light, and the wisdom of
God is the oil.
If it is lit, you are alive,
and if it is darkened,
you are dead.'

Zhang Zai

(1020–77)

'Heaven is my father and Earth is my mother, and even such a small creature as I finds an intimate place in their midst. Therefore that which extends throughout the universe I regard as my body and that which directs the universe I consider as my nature. All people are my brothers and sisters, and all things are my companions.'

'Western Inscription'

Zhang Zai was born in Hengqu, Shaanxi Province, and as a young man studied the works of Confucius. He then abandoned them, in favour of Buddhist and Daoist teachings, convinced that they would show him the right way to live. In the end, he turned back to Confucius, though his thinking was now informed by Buddhism and Daoism, and became one of the early forces behind the Neo-Confucianism revival of the Song dynasty.

According to Zhang, all things in the world are composed of *qi*, a primordial substance that includes both matter and the forces that determine the interplay between matter, *yin* and *yang*. *Qi* is not created or destroyed; instead it goes through a continuous process of condensing (*yin*) and dispersing (*yang*). When dispersed, it is invisible and insubstantial, but when it condenses it becomes a solid or a liquid and assumes new properties. All material things are composed of condensed *qi*: rocks, trees and even people. Everything is *qi*, everything shares the same essence, which is an idea that has important ethical implications, distinguishing Zhang's approach from the Buddhist focus on personal spiritual development divorced from this world.

In 1076 Zhang finished his major work, *Correcting Ignorance*, and presented it to his followers. The short statement known as the 'Western Inscription' – so called because it was displayed on the western wall of his study – was originally part of this larger work. In it, by asserting the essential unity of all things and the sense of mutual responsibility that this implies, Zhang was summarizing the main ethical position of Neo-Confucianism.

Averroes

(1126–98)

'Truth does not oppose
truth but accords with it
and bears witness to it.'

Decisive Treatise

Averroes – from the Arabic Ibn Rushd – was born in Cordoba, at the western edge of the Islamic world, into a family of distinguished jurists. He too became a judge, first in Cordoba and then in Seville, before basing himself in Marrakech, where he was the caliph's doctor. He wrote on a range of subjects, including jurisprudence and medicine, but it is for his philosophical contributions that he is best known today.

Based on Arabic translations, Averroes produced summaries of and detailed commentaries on the works of Aristotle. His aim was to present the most authentic version of Aristotelian thought possible in order to counter attacks against philosophy as a whole from Islamic jurists and theologians, whose arguments, he felt, were based on misreadings.

For Averroes, there was no intrinsic conflict between philosophy and the Qur'an as both of them revealed the truth and therefore supported each other; what's more, Muslims of intelligence and integrity had a positive duty to study philosophy, as it could only enhance their faith. For the rest, well, all the common people needed to know was that Islam is the best of all religions and, in line with Aristotelian ethics, produces the greatest happiness through a knowledge of God.

ZHu Xi

(1130–1200)

'**If one could but truly practise love and maintain it, one would possess the well-spring of all virtues and the root of all good deeds.**'

'A Treatise on Humanity'

Zhu Xi was born in Fujian Province and by the age of nineteen had passed the imperial exams for entry into the civil service. A Confucian scholar, he went on to become one of the most influential Neo-Confucians in China and beyond, his influence spreading to Korea, Japan and Vietnam. Where other scholars focused solely on Confucius's 'Five Classics', and in particular the *I Ching*, Zhu wrote commentaries on the later 'Four Books' – *The Analects*, *The Book of Mencius*, *The Great Learning* and *The Doctrine of the Mean* – considering them fundamental to a clearer understanding of Confucian thought.

For Zhu, Confucius's ethics centred on the cultivation and practice of *ren* (humaneness), which he defines as 'the essential character of mind' and 'the essential pattern of love'. In 'A Treatise on Humanity', he links *ren* with the cosmic urge to create, suggesting that all human concerns result from the creative impulse of heaven and earth. This, he says, is evident in the cycle of the seasons and the productiveness of nature as they support life. The drive to create exists everywhere, but only in humans is it distilled as *ren*, which, when fully realized, means caring for and acting responsibly towards others.

Zhu is credited with bringing back to the fore Confucius's original concern with individual ethical cultivation and practice after years of the more bureaucratic, careerist approach taken by generations of exam-passing Confucians.

Dōgen

(1200–1253)

'To study the self is
to forget the self.
To forget the self is to be
enlightened by all things.'

'Genjōkōan', *Shōbōgenzō*

The founder of the Sōtō school of Zen Buddhism and the Eihei Temple, both of which continue to thrive, Dōgen is Zen's foremost philosopher and also one of Japan's most influential thinkers. Zen has its roots in India, the original home of the Buddha, and China, where mainstream Mahāyāna Buddhism was introduced in the sixth century CE, blending with the existing Daoism to create Chan Buddhism. It then spread to Korea, Vietnam and Japan – 'Zen' is the Japanese pronunciation of 'Chan', meaning 'meditation'.

As a young monk Dōgen could not understand why it was necessary to treat religious practice as such a gruelling, relentless path to enlightenment if, as Mahāyāna Buddhism holds, the Buddha-nature is already present, perfect and whole, in each of us. His answer was to see practice as a way not of reaching one's inner Buddha-nature but of revealing it. With this in mind, he taught *zazen* (just sitting) meditation. Dōgen's disciples were to sit quietly with no other end in mind than to embrace the enlightenment they had had all along.

In the collection of essays, or fascicles, known as *Shōbōgenzō* ('Treasury of the True Dharma Eye'), Dōgen's approach to enlightenment takes on a philosophical dimension since it has profound implications for both the relationship between time and existence and the nature of stability and change in the world.

Roger Bacon

(c.1220–92)

'**There are two modes of acquiring knowledge, namely, by reasoning and by experience.**'

Opus Majus (1267)

Roger Bacon studied and then taught at the universities of Oxford and Paris, both major academic centres at the time. He lectured on Aristotle at Oxford and in Paris added arithmetic, geometry and astronomy to his repertoire.

Around 1247 Bacon returned to Oxford, keen to develop his interest in languages and experimental science. By 1257 he was a Franciscan friar, seeing this as no bar to his research, and true enough in 1266 Pope Clement IV asked him to put together a university study programme encompassing philosophy, science and languages, with the aim of consolidating the Church's teaching of theology and therefore its authority.

In the resulting *Opus Majus* (1267), Bacon trumpeted the virtues of experimental science, with its ability to discover new truths and verify conclusions. In place of outmoded authority, custom and ignorance, he proposed experiments that included calculating the position of heavenly bodies, reforming the calendar and creating telescopes. He also identified the colour spectrum, discussed the manufacture of gunpowder and outlined the possibility of flying machines. This flurry of excitement was short-lived, however. The pope died in 1268 and with him went the Church's enthusiasm for educational reform. By 1278 Bacon's work, now considered 'suspected novelties', led to his imprisonment. So much for the partnership between religion and science ...

Born into a noble family, Thomas Aquinas was educated in the Benedictine monastery at Monte Cassino and the University of Naples. He then joined the Dominicans and he went on to study in Cologne and Paris before Pope Alexander IV invited him back to teach in Italy.

By the thirteenth century the new universities – Paris was established in 1150 and Oxford in 1167 – were flourishing as centres of learning, independent of religious establishments. This coincided with the reappearance in the West of the works of Aristotle, translated from the Arabic commentaries of Avicenna and Averroes. Where Christianity sought knowledge through faith and divine revelation, Aristotle favoured reasoning. Aquinas combined both in a system that remains at the heart of Christian philosophy.

He accepted that faith and reason were separate, but considered them complementary. While specific doctrines, such as the Trinity and the Incarnation, were revealed through faith, Aquinas identified 'five ways', or proofs, for the existence of God in *Summa Theologica* (1265–74) using Aristotelian logic. God is the 'prime mover', bringing about motion in others; the first cause, triggering all other things; the necessary non-contingent being that precedes the existence of all contingent things; the greatest being from whom lesser things derive their relative greatness; and the intelligent designer who directs the actions of non-intelligent things. In addition, there were five statements about the divine nature of God, four cardinal virtues and three theological virtues. Sorted ...

THomas Aquinas

(1225–74)

'**Hence it was necessary for the salvation of man that certain truths which exceed human reason should be made known to him by divine revelation.**'

Summa Theologica (1265–74)

William of Ockham

(c.1287–1347)

'No more things should be presumed to exist than are absolutely necessary.'

The Franciscan friar William of Ockham was, like Thomas Aquinas, a major philosophical figure during the Middle Ages, furthering debates around Aristotle and scholasticism.

These days William's name is most commonly associated with the maxim Ockham's razor, which basically states that explanations should be kept as simple as possible. There is nothing to suggest that William was the first to propose this idea, or used this exact wording given here, but it fits well with the philosophical approach for which he is best known: metaphysical nominalism.

In *Summa Logicae* (c.1323), he challenged Aristotle's belief in the existence of universal essences or forms, considering them groundless and unnecessary complications when it came to understanding the world. Instead William saw only individual substances and individual qualities that people were aware of through 'intuitive cognition'. Anyone thinking about groups of things might use general terms, but these were only mental constructs, mere names – hence nominalism (from the Latin *nomen*, meaning 'name'). William also believed there was no way that logic could demonstrate the existence of God, whatever the Church said. For him belief was a matter of faith – and he had that faith. Again, the rule was keep it simple.

Desiderius Erasmus

(c.1469–1536)

'It is wisdom in
prosperity, when all
is as thou wouldst
have it, to fear and
suspect the worst.'

Proverbs or Adages (1545)

The great Renaissance scholar Desiderius Erasmus of Rotterdam bridges the medieval and modern worlds. Although he joined an Augustinian monastery in 1487 and was ordained a priest in 1492, he was soon dissatisfied with the prevailing system of philosophy and theology known as scholasticism, which was based on Aristotelian logic and the writings of the early Church Fathers. Looking back was key, tradition and dogma were paramount – no one was required to think any further.

Deciding that he was unsuited to monastic life, Erasmus was drawn to the humanists, with their belief in people's capacity for self-improvement and the importance of education. He travelled widely, teaching, writing and discussing ideas with Europe's leading intellectuals. For all his rejection of scholasticism, he had no desire to overturn the Church establishment. Rather, he favoured Christian humanism, with the best classical traditions of critical analysis meeting the best of Christian thought in a form of rational piety – a 'philosophy of Christ'. With this in mind, he prepared accurate versions of classical texts and edited the first printed New Testament in Greek.

The advent of the printing press meant that Erasmus could support himself through his scholarship. He was fascinated by proverbs, with their ability to convey simple truths in memorable ways, and his *Adagia* (*Proverbs or Adages*) appeared in ever-expanding versions. The one quoted here, from a 1545 edition, speaks loud and clear down the years in these times of pandemic.

Yi Hwang, also known as Toegye, was born in Gyeongsang Province, South Korea. The family fell on hard times when his mother was widowed before his first birthday, but she encouraged him to study and he mastered Confucius's *Analects* in his teens, in preparation for a civil service career. He then continued with the works of the Neo-Confucians, influenced in particular by Zhu Xi, and had no trouble excelling in the examinations.

Throughout his life, Yi Hwang was torn between government service and the desire to concentrate on his own scholarly and spiritual development. Towards the end of his life he struck a balance with *Ten Diagrams on Sage Learning* (1568), which he compiled as an instruction manual on how to achieve wisdom for King Seonjo.

Using past sages as role models of best practice, each of the ten chapters began with a diagram and a text from one of these earlier authorities, then concluded with a brief commentary by Yi Hwang. The first five chapters looked outwards, covering the workings of the universe and of society. The last five turned inwards and dealt with self-improvement, or the 'learning of the mind and heart', covering study of the inner life and ascetic practice.

Yi Hwang

(1501–70)

'The Confucian way of learning is that in order to ascend to lofty heights one must begin with the lowly, to travel afar one must begin with what is near.'

Ten Diagrams on Sage Learning (1568)

Yi I

(1536–84)

'Holding together
knowledge and action,
uniting what is internal
and external, one enters
the grounds of wisdom.'

Anthology of Wisdom Learning (1575)

Yi I, also known as Yulgok, was born in Gangwon Province, South Korea, into a family with a proud record of government service. Unlike his older contemporary Yi Hwang, he enthusiastically embraced a political career throughout his life, while at the same time establishing himself as a major Neo-Confucian thinker. The two men's different attitudes to public service were played out in the Four–Seven Debate, which concerned the moral nature of the mind and its emotions.

Two thousand years earlier, Mencius had written of the 'Four Sprouts': compassion, shame, respect and the sense of right and wrong – the innate moral sensibilities that underpinned the desired qualities of benevolence, righteousness, propriety and wisdom. Other Neo-Confucian texts described the 'Seven Feelings' that all humans are capable of experiencing: joy, anger, grief, fear, love, hate and desire. When these emotions are expressed, harmony ensues; when they are not, the result is equilibrium.

According to Yi Hwang, while the Four Sprouts were based purely in *li* (principle) and therefore were nothing but good, the Seven Feelings, which could be prompted by external events, included *qi* (material force) and were therefore both good and bad. For Yi I, however, principle cannot operate without material force and vice versa. In other words, he favoured a more practical, pragmatic approach that took account of external experience – ideas that he carried into his political career.

THomas HoBBes

(1588–1679)

> '**The life of man [is] solitary, poor, nasty, brutish, and short.**'

Leviathan (1651)

Educated at Oxford and tutor to the Cavendish family, earls of Devonshire, Thomas Hobbes had access to some of the leading intellects of the day. His interests ranged widely but it was not until the publication of *Leviathan* (1651) that he finally brought together all his thoughts on metaphysics, psychology and political philosophy.

A materialist, Hobbes saw the world as a mechanical system containing bodies in motion, driven by forces of attraction and repulsion; this could be applied to human behaviour too, determining what we call good and evil. People are instinctively selfish and, left to their own devices, default to fighting – with nasty, brutish consequences, not to mention none of the advantages brought by industry, culture or society. Enlightened self-interest explains why individual rights should give way to a social contract establishing civil society for everyone's protection, with all the benefits that follow. To keep the machine of state working smoothly, however, the power exercised by the sovereign has to be absolute – that ceding of individual rights applies only to the common people.

René Descartes

(1596–1650)

'I think therefore I am.'

Discourse on Method (1637)

The starting point was doubt: how can we know what we think we know? The evidence of our senses is insufficient, because maybe we are being deceived. All that's certain is we're thinking: *cogito ergo sum*, I think therefore I am ... Descartes reasoned that all ideas as clear as this must be true, because otherwise the *cogito* would be untrue. Included among his clear ideas was God, who, as the perfect being, would not deceive us as to the materiality of the external world. Reason alone allows Descartes to reach this conclusion. In a less elevated way, he argues that though the properties of wax change when it is melted, it remains wax. That such knowledge comes from the mind, not the senses, encapsulates the concept of dualism: the split between the non-material, thinking mind and the material, mechanistic body.

For all his rationality, Descartes came unstuck when Queen Christina invited him to Stockholm. The Swedish queen wanted philosophy lessons, at 5 a.m., in the middle of winter. Descartes contracted pneumonia and was dead within six months.

Blaise Pascal

(1623–62)

'Man is only a reed,
the weakest thing
in nature; but he is
a thinking reed.'

Pensées (1670)

The Pascal family moved from Clermont-Ferrand, where Blaise was born, to Paris in 1630. There he was educated by his father, who worked as a supervisor of taxes and was also a highly proficient mathematician. The child turned out to be something of a genius, contributing to debates on Euclidean geometry in his teens, inventing a mechanical calculating machine (later known as the Pascaline) and, in his correspondence with fellow mathematician Pierre de Fermat, laying the foundations of modern probability theory.

If ever there was a thinking reed it was Pascal. During a short life plagued by ill health, he did not publish any philosophical works, but he made major contributions to mathematics, physics and religious thought, all of them underpinned by a coherent line of philosophical reasoning. Pascal shared the mind–body dualism of his contemporary Descartes but not his rationalism; nor did he favour empiricism. Instead, he argued that while truths can be derived from earlier truths, first principles themselves are intuitive and cannot be proved. His answer was fideism – the idea that faith is independent of and superior to reason.

Published posthumously in 1670, *Pensées de M. Pascal sur la religion et sur quelques autres sujets* is a collection of notes that formed his reasoned defence of Christianity. Here probability theory and religious belief come together in Pascal's famous 'wager', in which he suggests that it is only rational to believe in God because if he exists we can look forward to happy-ever-after, and if he doesn't, well, we have not lost anything.

Baruch Spinoza

(1632–77)

'True virtue is nothing
else but living in
accordance with reason.'

Ethics (1677)

While Baruch Spinoza earned his living as a lens grinder, his true love was the study of ideas: he corresponded with other philosophical and scientific writers and produced his own works. Although his views were widely discussed, only the innocuous-sounding *Principles of Descartes' Philosophy* (1663) appeared under his name during his lifetime; *Theologico-Political Treatise* (1670) came out anonymously and *Ethics* (1677), his greatest work, was not published until just after his death.

As the Latin title, *Ethica Ordine Geometrica Demonstrata*, suggests, Spinoza felt that a complete ethical system could be drawn up on mathematical principles. The book ranged from God, through nature and its origins, to the emotions and the intellect. In it he rejected the mind–body dualism of René Descartes, seeing both as part of a continuous reality in nature, which equates with the universe, which equates with God – infinite and perfect. For Spinoza, God is not a personal creator but rather a pantheistic nature, with no interest in the fate of individuals. If humans think they have free will that is because they are ignorant of what causes their reactions.

In his analysis of the most useful approach to society, religion and the good life, Spinoza concludes that virtue – that is, happiness and well-being – lies not in a life ruled by transitory passions, or blind adherence to superstitions that pass for religion, but rather in the life of reason.

Having grown up against the backdrop of civil war, John Locke went to study at Oxford, where he pursued interests in medicine and experimental science. In 1667 he started to work for the prominent politician Lord Ashley as both a doctor and a scientific and political adviser. Considering it prudent because of his radical views to leave the country in the mid-1670s, he went to France and then the Netherlands, where he remained until after the Glorious Revolution of 1688, which replaced the autocratic James II with the constitutional monarchs William and Mary.

The first of Locke's major philosophical works, *Two Treatises of Government* (1689), argued that individuals naturally have the right to protect their life, health and property. They come together with others to form governments, whose duty it is to protect those rights. Governments become illegitimate if they fail to fulfil their side of the contract; no room here for the divine right of kings – the idea that monarchs are above the law, being God's representatives on earth.

All of which justified the Glorious Revolution and was of considerable interest to later revolutionaries in America and France.

John Locke

(1632–1704)

'The end of law is, not
to abolish or restrain,
but to preserve and
enlarge freedom.'

Second Treatise of Government (1689)

GOTTFRIED WILHELM LEIBNIZ

(1646–1716)

'It follows from the supreme perfection of God, that in creating the universe he has chosen the best possible plan, in which there is the greatest variety together with the greatest order; the best arranged ground, place, time; the most results produced in the most simple ways; the most of power, knowledge, happiness and goodness in the creatures that the universe could permit.'

The Principles of Nature and Grace (1714)

Gottfried Wilhelm Leibniz was born in Leipzig, where his father was professor of moral philosophy. He studied philosophy at the university there and jurisprudence at Altdorf, before being employed by the Elector of Mainz in 1667. His interests ranged widely: as well as codifying laws, drafting proposals for the unification of Protestants and Catholics, and serving as a courtier and diplomat, he played an active part in current mathematical, scientific and philosophical developments.

Like René Descartes and Baruch Spinoza, Leibniz favoured a rationalist approach where philosophy was concerned – mind over matter. Keen to come up with a system that reconciled a perfect God with the imperfect world, he proposed his sufficient-reason principle: everything exists exactly as it does for good reason.

The argument goes that for each individual there is a complete roadmap, known only to God, containing all their history. As God is perfect, each individual must be following a perfect plan. Underpinning this system are what Leibniz calls monads (from the Greek *monos*, meaning 'alone') – non-material unities, independent of each other, that evolve in a way predetermined by their nature. Each monad is a mirror of the universe and God has willed them into being.

Mary Astell

(1666–1731)

'If all Men are born free,
how is it that all Women
are born Slaves?'

Some Reflections upon Marriage (1700)

Born in Newcastle upon Tyne into a prosperous merchant family that then fell on hard times, Mary Astell was educated by her uncle, a clergyman who had studied philosophy and theology at Cambridge. She arrived in London in her twenties and had soon established herself within a group of well-connected freethinking women in favour of women's education.

Astell is remembered mainly as a proto-feminist, but her interests are rooted in those early studies with her uncle, and she corresponded with John Locke and George Berkeley on philosophical issues. In her two-part *A Serious Proposal to the Ladies* (1694, 1697), she followed René Descartes in arguing that all knowledge is based on reason, but said that to exclude women from education condemns them to being forever dismissed as empty-headed; they are conditioned, not born that way. Contemplation of pure ideas is the answer, their abstract nature leading the mind away from the senses to focus on an immaterial 'good'. For Astell, that immaterial good was God, and by combining the law of God and reason women could improve their understanding and so liberate themselves.

In *Some Reflections upon Marriage* (1700), she argued that since the marriage contract required absolute obedience to her husband – no social contract here – a woman must be convinced of his moral superiority. In other words, choose well or don't marry.

Born in Kilkenny, George Berkeley was educated at Trinity College Dublin, becoming a fellow in 1707. He remained at the university until 1713, during which time he was ordained a priest. His main philosophical works – *Essay towards a New Theory of Vision* (1709), *A Treatise Concerning the Principles of Human Knowledge* (1710) and *Three Dialogues between Hylas and Philonous* (1713) – were published at this relatively early stage in his career.

Berkeley was a leading proponent of idealism, believing that material objects do not exist independently of us. We might think we perceive them, but what we are actually perceiving is ideas and sensations. There is no way of verifying the existence of anything out there in three-dimensional space. So, when we perceive a table, we have a mental sensation, which is the idea of a table, made up of impressions from our senses, nothing more. The mind is necessary first: 'ESSE is PERCIPI' (to be is to be perceived), in Berkeley's words. So, does the table stop existing if we are not there? Berkeley felt that as long as it was being perceived it continued to exist, and who better than the all-seeing God to fulfil that role?

With religious enthusiasm to the fore, Berkeley focused his energies on plans to establish a university in Bermuda and spread the gospel 'among the American savages', but the promised funds failed to appear.

George Berkeley

(1685–1753)

'All the choir of heaven
and furniture of earth
– in a word, all those
bodies which compose
the mighty frame of the
world – have not any
subsistence without a mind.'

*A Treatise Concerning the Principles
of Human Knowledge* (1710)

Montesquieu

(1678–1755)

'Laws, in their most general signification, are the necessary relations arising from the nature of things. In this sense all beings have their laws: the Deity His laws, the material world its laws, the intelligences superior to man their laws, the beasts their laws, man his laws.'

The Spirit of Laws (1748)

Born into the aristocracy at the family château, Charles-Louis de Secondat, Baron de la Brède et Montesquieu, or simply Montesquieu, studied law in Bordeaux before heading to Paris.

His book *Persian Letters* (1721) was published anonymously to great success and marked the start of a literary career formulating his philosophy of political history. After three years visiting other countries to familiarize himself with different cultures and styles of government, Montesquieu began work. In *Considerations on the Causes of the Greatness of the Romans and Their Decline* (1734), he praised Republican Rome, seeing the empire as a decline into despotism. With *The Spirit of Laws* (1748), he widened his study to analyse the role played in a country's type of government by their customs and practices and even their climate. In conclusion, he identified three types: republics, where the people have sovereign power and the spirit, or guiding principle, is virtue; monarchies, where one person rules by established laws and the spirit is honour; and despotic regimes, where one person rules without laws and the spirit is fear.

With his denunciation of despotism, Montesquieu is seen as an early theorist of political freedom. For him, this was to be found in moderate governments, where power was shared between the legislature, the executive and the judiciary, and his ideas were enthusiastically taken up by the authors of the American constitution.

Voltaire

(1694–1778)

'**Superstition sets
the whole world
in flames; philosophy
quenches them.**'

Philosophical Dictionary (1764)

François-Marie Arouet was born in Paris and educated at the best Jesuit seminary in town. Determined to be a writer, he produced satirical verse and historical dramas from a young age, but even as he achieved success he was flirting with danger, attacking both religious and political authorities. On occasion he was forced to leave Paris for his own safety; he was imprisoned in the Bastille (changing his name to Voltaire while there) and in 1726 was exiled to England, staying for over two years.

He was much taken with England's liberal spirit, which he saw as being rooted in the civil liberties and constitutional monarchy that contrasted so sharply with the situation in France, where the aristocracy and the Catholic Church had a stranglehold on power. He was attracted by the empiricism of the scientist Isaac Newton and the works of John Locke, whose rational approach could counter the ignorance and superstition he identified in his own country.

Back in Paris Voltaire published *Philosophical Letters on the English Nation* (1733), which expressed these views with such gusto that he was forced to flee yet again. Undeterred, wherever he was based he continued producing works of non-fiction and fiction, drama and verse, together with thousands of letters. He never put forward an original philosophy, but rather used his writing – especially the *Philosophical Dictionary* (1764) – to challenge superstition and prejudice and promote religious toleration. A deist rather than a fan of organized Christian religion and a champion of reason, Voltaire embodied the ideals of the Enlightenment through his work: as he said, 'I write to act.'

David Hume

(1711–76)

'Reason is, and ought only to be the slave of the passions, and can never pretend to any other office than to serve and obey them.'

A Treatise of Human Nature (1739)

Born in Edinburgh, David Hume tried his hand at the law and in trade before heading to France in 1734. There he worked on his first and most important book, *A Treatise of Human Nature* (1739). He proposed a complete philosophical system that built on the scientific approach of earlier empiricists such as John Locke and George Berkeley to answer the basic question: how do we know what we know?

Hume argued that perceptions can be either impressions, which strike the mind with force (sensations, passions and emotions), or ideas, which are their faint echoes (thinking and reasoning). There is no other source of knowledge. And he is sceptical about reason: it is only habit that makes us look for real objects. The same goes for believing that the sun will come up tomorrow because it came up today; or seeing cause and effect in linked events. We accept these positions for practical purposes, but rather than worrying about ultimate reality, divine or otherwise, we should concentrate on experience and observation.

Jean-Jacques Rousseau

(1712–78)

> 'Man is born free, but he
> is everywhere in chains.'
>
> *The Social Contract* (1762)

Born in the Calvinist city of Geneva, Jean-Jacques Rousseau
had a miserable start in life, his mother dying there and
then. Ten years later his father fled to avoid imprisonment,
consigning the boy to the rather haphazard care of an uncle.

Rousseau believed, despite his early experiences, that
people are born happy and free, and would remain so
if left in a natural state. Once modernity encroached,
though, advances in the arts and sciences brought with
them inequality, misery and violence. His book *The Social
Contract* (1762) was an attempt to solve the problem of how
people could flourish socially and politically while retaining
freedom and avoiding chains. Rousseau's answer was a
contract whereby individuals surrendered their natural rights
to the collective 'general will', the only source of legitimate
sovereignty, which would then represent the common good.
No society could be equal and free – not to mention free
from violence – unless and until everyone accepted that the
general will was paramount.

Adam Smith

(1723–90)

'How selfish soever man may be supposed, there are evidently some principles in his nature, which interest him in the fortune of others, and render their happiness necessary to him, though he derives nothing from it except the pleasure of seeing it.'

The Theory of Moral Sentiments (1759)

Adam Smith was born in Kirkcaldy and from the age of fourteen attended the University of Glasgow. By 1748 he was delivering public lectures for the Philosophical Society of Edinburgh, mixing with the likes of David Hume. In 1751 he became professor of logic at Glasgow and shortly afterwards professor of moral philosophy, a position he held until 1764.

In 1759 Smith published *The Theory of Moral Sentiments*, in which he argued that the basis for moral behaviour is sympathy for the predicaments of others. He suggested that we have within us something like an impartial and well-informed spectator, judging others more objectively than we might be able to judge ourselves – he called it the 'invisible hand'. Smith had faith in the soundness of ordinary people's judgements and saw no need to seek overarching theoretical systems beyond that.

The same thread runs through his *Wealth of Nations* (1776). Rather than being a fixed stash of gold, wealth is created by trade and division of labour. We are all self-interested – not selfish, just looking out for ourselves. We improve our condition by producing goods and services that others want, benefiting them in the process. Governments do not need to make economic decisions for us because the invisible hand is already at work.

Immanuel Kant was born in Königsberg and spent his whole life there, studying and teaching at the university, where he eventually became professor of logic and metaphysics in 1770. Having originally lectured in mathematics and physics, he was determined to apply scientific methods to philosophy and come up with universal laws.

His fundamental idea was that, rather than operating as a blank canvas waiting for perceptions to make their mark, the human mind is actively engaged in acquiring knowledge, ordering and structuring material into intelligible categories. Knowledge of the world therefore depends on the structure of our mind, not on the structure of what we perceive. Concepts such as time and space or cause and effect are not learned from experience but are ways to make sense of the world. Kant compared the impact of his approach for philosophy to the revolution brought about by the astronomer Nicolaus Copernicus when he proved that the sun and not the earth was the centre of the universe.

Kant spoke of being filled with awe by 'the starry heavens above me and the moral law within me' – words that are on his tombstone. He believed that as well as a law of nature there is a moral law, and it was in *Fundamental Principles of the Metaphysics of Morals* (1785) that he identified the supreme moral law – his 'categorical imperative' – which is quoted here.

Immanuel Kant

(1724–1804)

'**Act only on that maxim whereby thou canst at the same time will that it should become a universal law.**'

Fundamental Principles of the Metaphysics of Morals (1785)

JoHann Herder

(1744–1803)

‘No one is in his age alone, he
builds on the preceding one,
this becomes nothing but the
foundation of the future, wants
to be nothing but that – this
is what we are told by the
analogy in nature, God's speaking
exemplary model in all works!’

*This Too a Philosophy of History
for the Formation of Humanity* (1774)

Johann Herder was born in Mohringen, Prussia, and in 1762 enrolled at the University of Königsberg, where he studied with Immanuel Kant. By 1764 he was a schoolteacher in Riga and he soon published his first philosophical essay, 'How Philosophy Can Become More Universal and Useful for the Benefit of the People' (1765). He began to focus on his writing, with works on literature and the origins of language and their role in forming national consciousness.

From his interest in the roots of language and culture, Herder developed a wider philosophy of history. He identified fundamental differences in people's beliefs, values and sensibilities from one historical period to another, seeing no reason to focus on great military leaders and their campaigns when studying people through their literature and arts would show them at their moral best.

In *This Too a Philosophy of History for the Formation of Humanity* (1774) Herder developed his thesis to suggest that history is one long chain of cultures that build on each other. Taking a human-scale approach and pulling together his different interests, he held that poetry evolved as a way of expressing deep emotions, using language that developed in complexity to express cultural values that had transformed over time – all as a way of confirming national identity.

Jeremy Bentham

(1748–1832)

'The greatest happiness of the greatest number is the foundation of morals and legislation.'

The Commonplace Book, in
The Works of Jeremy Bentham,
ed. John Bowring. Vol. X (1843)

Born in London, Jeremy Bentham showed early signs of a powerful intellect and was already studying at Oxford by the age of twelve. Following family tradition, he embarked on a career in the law, but he soon became disillusioned with the irrationality of existing legislation, finding 'no consistency, no harmony, no method whatever'. So, rather than practising, he determined to find ways to improve the whole legal system.

In *Introduction to the Principles of Morals and Legislation* (1789), Bentham developed ideas around the concept of utility – judging whether an action is right by measuring its tendency to produce 'benefit, advantage, pleasure, good, or happiness' or to prevent 'mischief, pain, evil, or unhappiness'. He used a 'felicific' or 'hedonistic calculus' to assess how likely something was to promote happiness, bearing in mind that one person's pleasure must not cause someone else's pain.

Still enthusiastic about legal reform, Bentham designed a new kind of prison, the panopticon, a circular building with a central observation tower from which prisoners could be – though possibly weren't being – watched. He felt this would encourage inmates to improve their behaviour, punishment being to prevent future harm rather than retribution for past offences. Applying his utilitarian approach to wider issues, Bentham argued against the existence of natural rights or duties, and social contracts. Such talk implied irrational appeals to a higher moral authority, but there was no authority above the law.

Born in Stuttgart and educated at Tübingen, Hegel was appointed a philosophy lecturer at Jena in 1801, then a professor in 1805, but after Napoleon's victory at the Battle of Jena in 1806 the university was closed. He worked as a newspaper editor and headmaster before, in 1818, becoming professor of philosophy at Berlin, which was fast becoming an intellectual centre with its emphasis on scientific progress. Hegel's lectures attracted great numbers of students from across Europe and his works provided inspiration for later radical thinkers, including Karl Marx.

Central to Hegel's philosophy is the idea of freedom, by which he meant not simply doing as you please but rather living in a fully aware way as part of a rationally organized society. *The Phenomenology of Spirit* (1807) outlines the development of consciousness, from basic awareness of phenomena via self-consciousness and reason to the pure consciousness of spirit, embracing reality itself, which he identified with knowledge of the Absolute. *The Science of Logic* (1812) explains how reality is revealed through dialectical reasoning: take a thesis, then its opposite – the antithesis – and the resulting conflict leads to synthesis. This underpins his move from 'being', via its opposite 'nothing', to 'becoming', when the mind knows itself fully and is free.

Hegel saw history as progressing the same way towards freedom. What he maybe failed to see was how political movements might be prepared to justify abuses in the name of historical imperative on the path to a glorious future.

Georg Wilhelm Friedrich Hegel

(1770–1831)

'The history of the world is none other than the progress of the consciousness of freedom.'

Introduction to *Lectures on the Philosophy of History* (1837)

Arthur Schopenhauer

(1788–1860)

'Every man takes the
limits of his own
field of vision for the
limits of the world.'

Studies in Pessimism (1851)

The son of a successful merchant, Arthur Schopenhauer was born in Danzig (now Gdansk) in Poland. He spent time at school in France and England before joining his father in business, but immediately regretted not opting for an academic career. When his father died suddenly, leaving him a sizeable inheritance, he took his chance and went off to study philosophy in Göttingen, Berlin and Jena.

The title of Schopenhauer's main work, *The World as Will and Representation* (1818), summarized his breakthrough insight. The world is one of representation: existing in space and time, it is made up of objects that we recognize through our consciousness. But beyond that consciousness there is more, for the world has its own inner being, what Schopenhauer calls the will, which is the spark for each representation. Outside of space and time, the will stands above knowledge and reason. Whatever other philosophers might think – he meant Hegel – the world is not a rational place. In fact, the will is positively irrational, and is the cause of all the frustrations we experience as we seek unattainable goals. Influenced by Eastern ideas, he advocated contemplation and the renunciation of desire, while also promoting the benefits of art and music.

From the start he disliked the Berlin academic establishment. As a junior lecturer, he deliberately scheduled his classes to clash with Hegel's – and had no students. Worse still, his book was ignored. He gave up teaching in disgust in 1831.

Auguste Comte

(1798–1857)

'The object of all true Philosophy is to frame a system which shall comprehend human life under every aspect, social as well as individual. It embraces, therefore, the three kinds of phenomena of which our life consists. Thoughts, Feelings, and Actions.'

A General View of Positivism (1848)

Born in Montpellier, in the south of France, Auguste Comte was educated in Paris at the École Polytechnique, which was established in 1794 – during the French Revolution – to train military engineers. Under Napoleon, it expanded to become France's foremost scientific institution, and for Comte, now France had emerged from the Napoleonic Wars, science was the way to provide the basis for an ideal society.

In 1826 Comte began to lecture to small groups of French thinkers and these lectures inspired his six-volume *Course of Positive Philosophy* (1830–42), as well as *A General View of Positivism* (1848). In them he explains that humanity goes through three stages of development: the theological, the metaphysical and the positive. In the first of these, while searching for absolute truths, people look to God to explain the phenomena around them. In the next, supernatural forces are replaced by abstract entities but the desire for definitive answers continues. Only in the final stage do people realize that they need to understand the scientific laws governing phenomena instead of worrying about their causes. This is Comte's positivism: only believe what can be scientifically verified or is capable of logical or mathematical proof.

Comte identified a new branch of science, 'sociology', that would manage the reorganization of ethics, politics and religion that was necessary to cement the new social order, and for a while positivist societies flourished in England and France.

Originally intending to become a clergyman, Ludwig Feuerbach changed his mind after reading the works of Hegel and went to study philosophy in Berlin instead. There he subsequently got involved with the Young Hegelians, radical thinkers who were convinced that Hegel's idea of history marching to its conclusion, guided by the twin goals of reason and freedom, was never going to come about while religion stood in its way.

In *The Essence of Christianity* (1841) Feuerbach set out to show that God is effectively a human invention, a spiritual construct to help people manage their hopes and fears. People project onto God all the good qualities they aspire to but often fail to achieve, seeing him as loving, compassionate and wise. The corollary is that while engaged in this wishful thinking, they neglect their own development – waiting for justice to be done in heaven rather than here on earth.

The book went on to inspire radical thinkers across Europe. According to Friedrich Engels, both he and Karl Marx felt that Feuerbach had a profoundly liberating effect on their ideas, establishing that human consciousness is the only sort of consciousness or spirit there is, and that it depends on the physical existence of people, who are part of nature. Which is a short step away from saying that religion is simply something used by those in power to oppress the rest, and distract them from reforms that are desperately needed.

Ludwig Feuerbach

(1804–72)

'**Religion is the dream of the human mind.**'

The Essence of Christianity (1841)

John Stuart Mill

(1806–73)

'It is better to be a human being dissatisfied than a pig satisfied; better to be Socrates dissatisfied than a fool satisfied.'

Utilitarianism (1863)

Born in London, John Stuart Mill was destined for great things according to his father, the Scottish philosopher and historian James Mill. Mill senior was a member of the Philosophical Radicals, supporters of Jeremy Bentham, and his son was to champion the utilitarian cause. With this in mind, the boy started studying Greek at three and then Latin so that he could master the philosophical classics; instruction in logic, political economy, history, law and philosophy followed.

A committed empiricist, he argued that external experience was the only reliable way to gain knowledge; relying on inner intuition instead would simply confirm existing prejudices. In *System of Logic* (1843), he proposed ways to improve the reliability of inductive reasoning, going from the particular to the general to come up with an approach as applicable to political, social and moral matters as to pure mathematics. In *On Liberty* (1859), his defence of the principle of freedom of thought and discussion, he argued that the only legitimate use of power was to prevent harm to others. This was no defence of abstract rights, however, more a conviction that as individuals pursued their own happiness they would together foster the general good of society.

Mill's ideas about the greater good were developed in *Utilitarianism* (1863), which proposed objective standards of good and right, equating them with the greatest happiness. Unlike Bentham, though, he saw a distinction between higher and lower pleasures, hence the quote here.

Harriet Taylor Mill

(1807–58)

'We deny the right of any
portion of the species to
decide for another portion
what is and what is not
their "proper sphere".
The proper sphere for all
human beings is the largest
and highest which they
are able to attain to.'

'The Enfranchisement of Women',
Westminster Review (1851)

Harriet Hardy was born in London into a well-established family and was educated at home before marrying John Taylor, a successful businessman, at the age of eighteen. Through their involvement with the Unitarian Church, the Taylors were at the centre of a group of radical thinkers, with Harriet an enthusiastic advocate of social reform, especially rights for women. William Johnson Fox, editor of the Unitarian journal *Monthly Repository*, for which Harriet Taylor wrote, introduced John Stuart Mill into their circle and this was the beginning of a lifelong collaboration. She separated from her husband and eventually married Mill; he credited her with co-authorship of his philosophical works.

That shared-authorship claim was disputed at the time and remains the subject of debate. However, it is accepted that Taylor Mill was the author of 'The Enfranchisement of Women', an essay published under Mill's name in July 1851 in *Westminster Review*, the journal founded by Jeremy Bentham. Here she argued that there was no justification for denying women equality in all areas of life; it was custom alone that restricted their actions to the domestic sphere, with men consigning them there. To deny women political agency meant they could not act for the greater good of society. Without equal access to education their moral and intellectual development suffered. She compared marriage to slavery, claiming that both relied on the threat of physical force, and called for laws against domestic violence.

Born in Besançon, in eastern France, Pierre-Joseph Proudhon had little formal education as a child, but his mother encouraged him to study and in 1827 he was apprenticed to a printer. In the course of his work correcting proofs, he met various authors and through them became interested in issues of current social, political and philosophical concern. In 1840 he published his first book, *What is Property? Or, an Inquiry into the Principle of Right and of Government*.

According to Proudhon, the straightforward answer to that question is theft. In saying this, he was arguing that when a worker sells either what they have made or their services, they should receive in return only money, goods or services that have equal economic value. In this form of mutualism, which was Proudhon's mix of socialism and anarchy, there is no room for anyone profiting from loans, investments or rent.

By referring to himself as an anarchist, Proudhon meant that he did not believe in the government of one group of people by another, in the same way that he did not believe in – and did not believe that anyone else would favour – the exploitation of one group by another. This held for religious leaders and capitalists as well as for politicians. He was looking for a society without authority, in which people owned only what they produced, acquiring the means of production through cooperatives and labour associations. Anarchy, for Proudhon, was 'order without power' and his ideas would prove very popular with radicals throughout Europe, and in Russia in particular.

Pierre-Joseph Proudhon

(1809–65)

'As man seeks justice in equality, so society seeks order in anarchy.'

What is Property? (1840)

Søren Kierkegaard

(1813–55)

'The crucial thing is to find a truth that is true for me, to find the idea I am willing to live and die for.'

Journal entry, 1 August 1835

Søren Kierkegaard was born into a wealthy family in Copenhagen, the youngest of seven children. His deeply religious, scholarly but melancholic father believed himself cursed by God, and the death of his wife and five children before Søren reached twenty-one did not help.

Kierkegaard studied theology at Copenhagen University, initially intending to pursue a career in the Church, but he became more interested in philosophical debate within the academic world and took up writing instead. Positioning himself against the dominant German idealist philosophy of the day, he disagreed vehemently with Hegel's view that life was as a rational progression from simple consciousness through reason to absolute knowledge. For Kierkegaard, this put man in the place of God, ignoring the subjective and limited standpoint from which human judgements are necessarily made. Rather, he emphasized the importance of freedom of choice.

Kierkegaard's books explore different ways of living once individual responsibility is accepted. The results are not comfortable. In *Either/Or* (1843), he contrasts the short-term pleasures of the aesthetic life with the moral grounding of the ethical one; the former leads only to dread and despair. In *The Concept of Anxiety* (1844), he turns again to dread and despair, this time as experienced in the face of choice. But as the journal entry quoted here shows, he had already taken his first steps towards accepting individual responsibility a decade earlier; and years later he would serve as an inspiration to the existentialists.

Karl Marx

(1818–83)

'**Philosophers have hitherto only *interpreted* the world in various ways; the point is to *change* it.**'

'Theses on Feuerbach' (1845)

Best known now as the author (with Friedrich Engels) of *The Communist Manifesto* (1848) and *Capital* (1867), Karl Marx started out as a philosopher, studying at the universities of Bonn and Berlin. In Berlin, he was influenced by the Young Hegelians, a group who developed Hegel's idea that reason and freedom determined the path of history. Whereas Hegel saw his own time as the triumphant end of history, the Young Hegelians felt there was further to go as political and religious freedoms still remained elusive. Hegel's dialectical approach needed refinement.

Unlike Hegel, for whom the real world was simply the external manifestation of the Absolute, Marx put the material world and the human mind centre stage. We humans produce what we need to survive. We are what we produce and our nature is determined by our material condition. Marx saw human history as a succession of economically driven class conflicts, with each societal stage generating forces that would destroy it, with a new version emerging from the ashes. Economic development (thesis) meets revolutionary violence (antithesis), leading to a fairer future (synthesis).

Marx took philosophy out into the world, with repercussions that continue to this day. The Eleventh Thesis on Ludwig Feuerbach, quoted here, appears on his tombstone in Highgate Cemetery, London, together with the last line of *The Communist Manifesto*: 'Workers of all lands unite!'

Born in Derby into a nonconformist family, Herbert Spencer was influenced from an early age by the anti-establishment and anti-clerical views of his father, who was a teacher and also secretary of the Derby Philosophical Society. Largely self-taught, he published his first book, *Social Statics* (1851), while subeditor of *The Economist*, the free-trade newspaper still in print today, and through its publisher he met many of London's leading radical thinkers, including John Stuart Mill.

One of the most prolific and popular thinkers of his time, Spencer came up with the term 'survival of the fittest' after reading Charles Darwin's *On the Origin of Species* (1859), but he himself had already been working on ideas of evolution for some years. He developed what he called a 'system of synthetic philosophy', aiming to demonstrate how evolution operated in the worlds of biology, psychology and ethics. Spencer saw life as a process of continuous adjustment so as to be better able to survive and, by extension, flourish.

The progression Spencer charted was from simple, hierarchical and aggressive societies to complex, cooperative and industrial ones as people sought stability and prosperity. This would happen organically, with minimal state intervention, as societies organized on the basis of 'liberty for each, limited by the like liberty of all'. Whatever the theory, the practice did not follow, Spencer's light faded and what became known as 'social Darwinism' was co-opted as justification for their methods by the unscrupulous.

Herbert Spencer

(1820–1903)

‘**Progress is not an accident, not a thing within human control, but a beneficent necessity.**’

Social Statics (1851)

CHarLeS Peirce

(1839–1914)

'The opinion which is fated to be ultimately agreed to by all who investigate, is what we mean by the truth, and the object represented in this opinion is the real. That is the way I would explain reality.'

'How to Make Our Ideas Clear',
Popular Science Monthly (1878)

The son of a Harvard professor of mathematics, Charles Peirce was encouraged to solve problems of logic by his father from a young age. His own degree was in chemistry, and after graduating he put his scientific and mathematical background to good use, making computations for the US Coast and Geodetic Survey for over three decades, while also teaching logic at Harvard for some years.

Peirce referred to himself as a 'laboratory philosopher', convinced that his practical experience was what led him to the philosophical approach he initially called pragmatism, which he explained in 'How to Make Our Ideas Clear' (1878). Philosophy can be treated like any experimental science, with logic, which he regarded as 'the art of devising methods of research', firmly rooted in objective experience of the world. To investigate a problem we propose a theory, assuming it to be true but knowing that its truth depends on testing. Truth, and therefore meaning, are bound up with what happens next. Theories are confirmed by their consequences, those nearer the truth – for there are no objective certainties – being the ones that surpass their rivals in helping us to understand the world.

Peirce believed that clarity of meaning was all-important – clarity about the concept under discussion, its constituent parts and the implications of its effects. Once he decided that pragmatism's meaning had been diluted, he simply came up with a variant: pragmaticism.

William James

(1842–1910)

'The art of being wise
is the art of knowing
what to overlook.'

The Principles of Psychology (1890)

William James, older brother of the novelist Henry, was born into a wealthy and cultured New York family. After studying medicine at Harvard, he embarked on a career teaching and writing about psychology and philosophy. In his two-volume *Principles of Psychology* (1890) James established the importance of not only a scientific approach to experimental psychology but also a coherent philosophical framework within which to set results as they are experienced.

That philosophy was explained in *Pragmatism* (1907), where James took Charles Peirce's idea that a concept's meaning consists of its practical consequences and then applied it to his own particular fields of interest. For James, philosophies are more than hard-edged intellectually honed theories; they also represent groundswells of feeling, so that aiming for precision is pointless and challenging other people's work by refuting particular statements is no more effective than trying to halt the course of a river by placing a few logs in there (James is the man who came up with the idea of 'the stream of consciousness').

Both James and Peirce saw pragmatism as a way of clarifying concepts and hypotheses, but where Peirce was grounded solely in science, James felt that people need a philosophy that, while adhering to scientific facts, still finds room for faith and human values. For him, pragmatism was that middle way, reconciling the two.

Born in Saxony, Friedrich Nietzsche studied theology and philology at the University of Bonn. However, while there he lost his faith, convinced that science and secular reasoning undermined religion. Concentrating on philology instead, he became professor at the University of Basel when only twenty-four.

Nietzsche's philosophical interests were unconventional. He was not concerned with theories about the nature of knowledge; instead, he wanted to understand why people act as they do. In *The Birth of Tragedy* (1872), he contrasted the 'Apollonian' and 'Dionysian' values of ancient Greece, suggesting that the order and reason of the former are mistakenly prized over the more spontaneous passions of the latter. As for Christianity, it is nothing but a denial of life-affirming instincts, promoting a 'slave morality'. In *Thus Spoke Zarathustra* (1883) and *Beyond Good and Evil* (1886), he proposed a new morality based on confident self-assertion, motivated by 'the will to power'. This was embodied in the Übermensch or superman, someone strong enough to break free of conventions, master his passions and direct his energies constructively in this world, not wait for the next.

In *Ecce Homo*, written in 1888 but not published until 1908, Nietzsche asserted that he had exposed the fraud that is the whole of Western philosophy and Christianity. As the quote suggests, he saw himself as a one-man Dionysian wrecking ball breaking down complacent bourgeois values.

Friedrich Nietzsche

(1844–1900)

'What I understand
by "philosopher":
a terrible explosive in
the presence of which
everything is in danger.'

Ecce Homo (1908)

Edmund Husserl

(1859–1938)

'Philosophy as science, as serious, rigorous, indeed apodictically rigorous science – *the dream is over.*'

The Crisis of European Sciences and Transcendental Phenomenology (1936)

Born in Moravia, Edmund Husserl studied mathematics, physics and philosophy in Berlin, then philosophy, psychology and logic in Vienna. He pulled all these subjects together in his first book, *Philosophy of Arithmetic* (1891), to suggest a psychological foundation for logic and arithmetic. On publication, the book was criticized by mathematicians for introducing subjectivity where it did not belong. Undeterred, Husserl developed a new philosophical method: phenomenology – literally the study of phenomena.

Husserl was interested in what determines the way we experience things: how they appear to us (via perception, thought, memory, emotion, etc.) and the meanings they have for us. Whereas other philosophical approaches assume that things, possessing their own essences, exist independently in the 'real' world, phenomenology starts with conscious experience from a subjective point of view.

Phenomenology was immediately different from other types of philosophy. Where ontology concerned itself with the nature of being, epistemology with the nature of knowledge, logic with valid reasoning and ethics with questions of right and wrong, phenomenology considered such issues as consciousness, first-person perspective and intentionality. These areas were to be of great interest to existentialist thinkers such as Martin Heidegger and Jean-Paul Sartre, but sadly, in *The Crisis of European Sciences and Transcendental Phenomenology* (1936), Husserl had to accept that his quest for a rigorous science to underpin the whole of philosophy was over.

John Dewey

(1859–1952)

'The moment philosophy supposes it can find a final and comprehensive solution, it ceases to be inquiry and becomes either apologetics or propaganda.'

Logic (1938)

In 1894 John Dewey was appointed chairman of the department of philosophy, psychology and pedagogy at the newly founded University of Chicago, where he refined his approach across all three areas. Ten years later he became professor of philosophy at Columbia, New York, staying there until he retired in 1930.

Linked philosophically with the pragmatism of Charles Peirce and William James, Dewey held that the true test of a proposition's validity is its consequences in the real world, the role of knowledge being to facilitate human purposes. Rather than passively absorbing knowledge, the mind interacts with its environment and adjusts its ideas accordingly. Again, with psychology, Dewey saw process and interaction instead of a fixed stimulus/response reaction. As for pedagogy, he established the University of Chicago Laboratory Schools, putting into practice his belief that education should foster children's natural inquisitiveness by imparting skills to help them learn through inquiry.

Nishida Kitarō

(1870–1945)

> 'Thus *pure experience* is synonymous with *direct experience*. When one experiences directly one's conscious state there is as yet neither subject nor object, and knowledge and its object are completely united. This is the purest form of experience.'

An Inquiry into the Good (1911)

Nishida Kitarō grew up at the start of the Meiji period, when Japan was opening itself to Western influences after years of isolationism. This meant that in school he studied not only Confucian, Neo-Confucian and Daoist classics, but also English and German, even tackling the works of Hegel and Kant.

His interest in Zen Buddhism developed at Tokyo University when he saw that Zen practice had relevance to discussions of realism and empiricism within Western philosophy. His interpretation of pure experience and self-awareness relates to the Zen emphasis on *satori* or enlightenment; his later philosophy of the *topos* or place of absolute nothingness that contains all reality, subjective and objective, references the Zen notion of emptiness; and his religious world-view takes in both God and Buddha.

D. T. Suzuki

(1870–1966)

'How hard, then,
and yet how easy it is
to understand Zen!
Hard because to
understand it is not
to understand it; easy
because not to understand
it is to understand it.'

An Introduction to Zen Buddhism (1934)

D. T. or Daisetz (Daisetsu) Teitarō Suzuki was born in Kanazawa, the capital of Ishikara Prefecture. Like his contemporary Nishida Kitarō, he grew up at the start of the Meiji period, when Japan was rapidly modernizing, and was keen to learn English and study Western thought. He attended Tokyo University, but also spent five years at Engakuji monastery in Kamakura, just south of Tokyo, engaged in Zen Buddhist practice.

One of a new generation of Japanese thinkers who wanted to reinterpret Buddhism for modern times, in 1897 Suzuki moved to America to work for a publishing company as a translator and editor. In 1909 he returned to Japan, eventually becoming a professor of Buddhist studies at Otani University, Kyoto. It was there that he started the journal *Eastern Buddhist* and published many of his most important books in English and Japanese. In *An Introduction to Zen Buddhism* (1934), he set out to explain that, rather than being a Western-style religion with a god to worship, ceremonial rites to observe and an immortal soul to worry about, or a specific school of philosophy, Zen embraces all philosophy and religion in its quest for personal development with a view to attaining *satori* or enlightenment.

After the Second World War, Suzuki returned to America as a visiting professor, remaining until 1958. During this time there was an enormous interest in Buddhism in the West and Suzuki was the authority as far as Western scholars and the wider public were concerned.

Bertrand Russell

(1872–1970)

'The man who has no tincture of philosophy goes through life imprisoned in the prejudices derived from common sense, from the habitual beliefs of his age or his nation, and from convictions which have grown up in his mind without the cooperation or consent of his deliberate reason.'

The Problems of Philosophy (1912)

Bertrand Russell was educated at Trinity College, Cambridge, where he studied first mathematics and then philosophy. Rejecting the neo-Hegelian idealism that was in vogue at the time, with its quest for overarching metaphysical systems, Russell focused instead on the logical analysis that underpins mathematics.

In *Principles of Mathematics* (1903), he argued that mathematics is effectively logic, derived from axioms that are objectively certain. The idea was expanded in the three-volume *Principia Mathematica* (1910–13), which he co-wrote with Alfred North Whitehead. Here they explained that the same analytical approach is applicable to questions of philosophy, breaking down complex notions into their constituent parts, but only if language and grammar can be clarified so that they are capable of expressing ideas clearly enough for them to become philosophical truths, as objectively certain as logical axioms. Their linguistic work paved the way for the approach taken by the logical positivists of the Vienna Circle, among others.

Russell's influence extended well beyond the academic world. He was able to convey complex ideas in clear language and published several popular science books, while his sweeping survey *History of Western Philosophy* (1945) is still in print today; he also won the Nobel Prize in Literature in 1950.

Born in London, G. E. Moore studied classics and then – encouraged by his friend Bertrand Russell – philosophy at Trinity College, Cambridge, where he was also a fellow from 1898 to 1904. After some time working independently at philosophy, in 1911 he returned to Cambridge as a lecturer and in 1925 was appointed professor of philosophy and logic. He also edited the influential philosophy journal *Mind* from 1921 to 1947.

Moore felt that philosophy needed to match the advances science had made, with an emphasis on exact meaning through careful use of language. He was in the forefront of a move away from the idealism currently in vogue in Britain, favouring a more analytical approach. As far as he could see, arguing that the nature of the world depends on our perceptions of it is illogical because its assumptions are far less convincing than the opinion that a real world of physical objects exists. The role of philosophy was not to prove the truth of common-sense beliefs but to consider their significance.

In his best-known work, *Principia Ethica* (1903), Moore refers to the naturalistic fallacy – the result of pointless attempts to define 'good', say, in terms of other qualities. He argues that good is a simple, indefinable, unanalysable property. Certain things can be identified as good – he singled out friendship and aesthetic experience – but to see good as having natural properties is mistaken.

G. E. Moore

(1873–1958)

'If I am asked "What is good?" my answer is that good is good, and that is the end of the matter. Or if I am asked "How is good to be defined?" my answer is that it cannot be defined, and that is all I have to say about it.'

Principia Ethica (1903)

Ludwig Wittgenstein

(1889–1951)

'What can be said at all
can be said clearly; and
whereof one cannot speak
thereof one must be silent.'

Preface to *Tractatus Logico-Philosophicus* (1922)

Ludwig Wittgenstein was born in Vienna into a large, wealthy family. Educated at home until he was fourteen, he finished his schooling in Austria before going on to study mechanical engineering in Berlin and Manchester. It was while doing research into aeronautics that he became interested in mathematics and then in the foundations of mathematics, at which point he changed tack and went to Cambridge to study mathematical logic with Bertrand Russell. Within two years, Russell announced there was nothing more he could teach Wittgenstein.

During the First World War Wittgenstein served in the Austrian army, but this did not stop his work on logic. He kept notebooks throughout the war and finished his first book in an Italian prisoner of war camp. Published in English as *Tractatus Logico-Philosophicus* (1922), this was the only book of his to appear in his lifetime.

According to Wittgenstein, for language to be meaningful, it must mirror states of affairs in the real world. This immediately disqualifies most conventional discourse – from value judgements to much speculative thought – making it literally meaningless. If the limits of language are indeed the limits of thought, we arrive at Wittgenstein's very logical conclusion (see opposite). But that silence also marks a dead end, so it's not surprising that Wittgenstein turned away from this line of reasoning, the *Tractatus* both opening and closing the first phase of his philosophical career.

Martin Heidegger

(1889–1976)

> ' We are ourselves the
> entities to be analysed.'

Being and Time (1927)

Martin Heidegger's major work, the unfinished *Being and Time* (1927), concerns 'the question of being' (*Seinsfrage*). Heidegger does not come at the problem via traditional philosophical discussions of epistemology, subjectivity, representation, objective knowledge and so on. His main focus is directly on humans and our sense of place in the world – he uses the term 'being there' (*Dasein*) or 'existence'. Being means to exist in the period between birth and death. Being is literally time and time is finite.

Only if we are constantly aware of the inevitability of our own death can we understand what it means to live as an authentic human being. We are free to choose our actions and to focus our energies within the world, but must all the while guard against modern technological developments that divorce us from the immediacy of being that was experienced by our ancestors. With his emphasis on authenticity and individual freedom, Heidegger would prove irresistible to the existentialists.

Feng Youlan

(1895–1990)

> ' The present should embrace
> all of the best of the past. '

Address given at Columbia University,
New York, 1982

Feng Youlan went to university in Shanghai and then Beijing to study Western philosophy and logic. He graduated in 1918 and won a scholarship to Columbia University, where he was much influenced by John Dewey. Returning to China in 1923, he published his first major work, *A History of Chinese Philosophy* (1934), which looked at Chinese philosophy through a Western, positivist lens. Next came *New Rational Philosophy* (1939), which was influenced by twelfth-century Neo-Confucianism.

Rejecting certain mystical elements of Daoism and Buddhism, which saw metaphysics in terms of spiritual development and enlightenment, the Neo-Confucians adopted a more secular approach, treating metaphysics as a way to formulate a humanistic philosophy in which individuals strive for a harmonious relationship with this world. Feng went further, applying Western positivist logic to come up with an ethical theory that accounted for both the nature of morality and individual moral development within that wider context.

Herbert Marcuse

(1898–1979)

' The people recognize themselves
in their commodities; they find
their soul in their automobile,
hi-fi set, split-level home, kitchen
equipment. The very mechanism
which ties the individual to his
society has changed, and social
control is anchored in the new
needs which it has produced. '

One-Dimensional Man (1964)

Herbert Marcuse was born in Berlin and studied at the university there, and also in Freiburg, before becoming very involved with the Frankfurt Institute of Social Research (the Frankfurt School). In 1934 he fled from Nazi Germany to New York, where the Institute was re-established, and began teaching at Columbia University. After the Second World War Marcuse stayed in the USA, teaching at Harvard, Brandeis and San Diego.

His first work in English, *Reason and Revolution* (1941), was a discussion of the social theories of Hegel and Marx, while *Eros and Civilization* (1955) put forward a Freudian analysis of the way capitalism operates by imposing restrictions on individuals that create barriers to the formation of a non-repressive society.

It was not until the publication of *One-Dimensional Man* (1964), however, that Marcuse struck a real chord with the emerging radical student movement, earning him the title 'Father of the New Left'. Here Marcuse argued against what he called the 'repressive tolerance' of modern industrial society, where the masses were both stimulated and satisfied, to the point of stupefaction, by the products of their own labour, at the expense of their more fundamental needs and freedoms. He looked to people outside the system – students, intellectuals and minorities – to initiate revolutionary change, which understandably appealed to those groups, but Marcuse's influence did not last long beyond the student riots of the 1960s in California and Paris.

FriedricH HayeK

(1899–1992)

'... the danger of tyranny
that inevitably results from
governmental control of
economic decision-making
through central planning ...'

The Road to Serfdom (1944)

Born and educated in Vienna, Friedrich Hayek became the director of the Austrian Institute for Economic Research in 1926. From 1931 to 1950, he taught at the London School of Economics, then moved to the universities of Chicago (1950–62) and Freiburg (1962–70). His name is associated with the Austrian School of economic thought, which advocated methodological individualism – the idea that economic and social developments result from the actions of individuals, not the imposition of large-scale macroeconomic theories.

Hayek took his economic ideas into the philosophical realm with *The Road to Serfdom* (1944), which considered the role of government in society. Linking the roots of fascism, Nazism and socialism, he asserted that central planning of any political stripe invariably involves compulsion and the systematic erosion of liberty. For Hayek, the problem is that those who set out to plan society can never have access to the knowledge necessary, because knowledge is not fixed or universally applicable; societies are always spontaneous, the result of individual actions not grand designs.

Hayek believed that personal and economic freedom are inseparable and that state intervention, even if well intentioned, undermines them. The only legitimate role for government, then, is to facilitate the market and to provide services that the market cannot provide itself. Hayek was awarded the Nobel Prize in Economic Sciences in 1974 and his ideas proved understandably popular with free-market governments everywhere.

Gilbert Ryle taught philosophy at Oxford before the Second World War, worked in intelligence during the war and then returned to the university to become Waynflete Professor of Metaphysical Philosophy at Magdalen College, a position he held from 1945 to 1968.

As a proponent of linguistic or 'ordinary language' philosophy, he saw his job as being to expose the sources of common misconceptions and nonsensical theories embedded in linguistic idioms that lead inexorably from small quirks to major logical errors. He pointed to 'category mistakes' that result in two grammatically linked things being treated as logical equivalents. An example he had fun playing with in *The Concept of Mind* (1949), his major work, was 'She came home in a flood of tears and a sedan-chair.'

Ryle used the same approach in the book to challenge what he referred to as philosophy's 'official doctrine' of Cartesian dualism, arguing that René Descartes' separation of mind and body into different categories is an idea that makes sense only in a time before our current understanding of biology. How can anyone seriously think about a human body that exists in time and space, that is subject to mechanical laws, and then come up with a mysterious entity that doesn't? To do so is to invent a ghost in the machine. For Ryle, the mind could now be seen as a set of capacities and abilities belonging to the body, an intrinsic working part, its intelligent behaviour. Descartes' ghost had well and truly been exorcized.

Gilbert Ryle

(1900–1976)

'... the ghost in the machine ...'

The Concept of Mind (1949)

Born in Vienna, capital of the Austro-Hungarian Empire, Karl Popper studied at the university there. By the time he graduated, the First World War was over and the empire was no more, but Vienna remained an intellectual centre, home to the logical positivists. Popper shared their interest in science, but considered it no more verifiable than ethics or metaphysics. Instead, he was interested in falsification.

In *The Logic of Scientific Discovery* (1934), Popper argued that science proceeds not by induction, with theories produced from repeated observations and proved by experiments, but by formulating new hypotheses and testing them rigorously. Experiments cannot prove but they can refute theories. There is nothing wrong in putting forward an interesting hypothesis that is then refuted; what is wrong is proposing a hypothesis that cannot be tested or adhering to one despite evidence to the contrary. So, science is provisional knowledge that advances by eliminating theories that are found to be false.

Popper's scientific philosophy had social and political implications too. Having left Austria for New Zealand in 1937 to avoid German occupation, in articles such as 'The Poverty of Historicism', *Economica*, Vols. 11 and 12 (1944–5), and books such as *The Open Society and Its Enemies* (1945) he challenged the idea that history was leading to an inevitable conclusion as an untestable, unscientific assertion used to justify oppression and fanaticism. Popper argued instead for open democratic societies that grow organically, without anyone trying to impose a new order ... yet again.

Karl Popper

(1902–94)

'It must be possible
for an empirical scientific
system to be refuted
by experience.'

The Logic of Scientific Discovery (1934)

Jean-Paul Sartre

(1905–80)

'Existence comes before essence.'

'Existentialism is a Humanism',
lecture given in Paris, 1945

Born in Paris, Jean-Paul Sartre attended the prestigious École Normale Supérieure, where he met his lifelong companion, fellow philosopher Simone de Beauvoir. His teaching career was interrupted by the Second World War, during which he spent nine months in a German prisoner of war camp. He was also active in the French Resistance. After the war he abandoned teaching to concentrate on spreading his philosophical and political ideas as widely as possible.

For Sartre the existentialist, there is no God, no omniscient creator with a plan, which means that humans exist before there is any conception of them – hence existence before essence. We come first, become aware of ourselves, engage with the world and define ourselves as we go, right until the very end. With no such thing as human nature, we are each of us alone, 'condemned to be free', with the terrifying prospect of being fully responsible for how we live.

These ideas were explored not only in philosophical works but also in novels and plays showing the consequences of the actions, or lack of action, taken by different characters. Sartre believed that writers have a duty to further social and political debate. He was a committed Marxist and an enthusiastic member of the radical New Left in France in the 1960s and 1970s.

Ayn Rand was born in St Petersburg but left for the USA in 1926, dissatisfied with life in the newly created Soviet Union. Her first books, *We the Living* (1936) and *Anthem* (1938), portray individualists who are ultimately destroyed by totalitarian regimes. The architect hero of *The Fountainhead* (1943), her next novel, refuses to bow to the authorities when expelled from college (the 'quote' here, though commonly cited, in fact conflates their dialogue) and never deviates from this path.

Rand's books were not well received by critics, but they obviously struck a chord with the public and *The Fountainhead* became a bestseller. Next to appear was *Atlas Shrugged* (1957), in which productive and creative individuals are failed by an incompetent system that supports lazy scroungers. Taken together, they formed the basis of a philosophy known as objectivism, which promoted single-minded individualism, rational self-interest and laissez-faire capitalism as the only way for the strong to thrive.

Rand's call for a minimal state whose only rationale is to protect the rights of the individual is echoed enthusiastically today by the libertarian political movement, which sees personal freedom – whether on the left or the right of the political spectrum – as more important than any idea of the collective good.

Ayn Rand

(1905–82)

'The question isn't who
is going to let me; it's who
is going to stop me.'

The Fountainhead (1943) ... almost

Hannah Arendt

(1906–75)

' ... the banality of evil ... '

Eichmann in Jerusalem (1963)

Born near Hannover into a secular Jewish family, Hannah Arendt studied philosophy and theology at Marburg, Freiburg and Heidelberg, where she was taught by three of the foremost thinkers of the time, Edmund Husserl, Martin Heidegger and Karl Jaspers. Aware that Germany was becoming increasingly unsafe for Jews, she moved to Paris in 1933 and then, in 1941, to New York.

Her first major work, *The Origins of Totalitarianism*, was published in 1951. Here she argued controversially that Stalin's communism and Hitler's Nazism were alike, both resulting from the collapse of political systems that had existed for years until the rise of nationalism, colonialism and racism in the nineteenth century, followed by the chaos of the First World War and the Great Depression. Totalitarian regimes offered simplistic solutions to complex problems, seducing people with their talk of the laws of history and destiny. Ideology had replaced morality, so that individuals were not called upon to think about their own political responsibilities towards others.

It was the trial of the Nazi war criminal Adolf Eichmann in Jerusalem in 1963 that brought her to wider attention. She was sent by the *New Yorker* to cover proceedings and that year published the book *Eichmann in Jerusalem*. In it she developed her earlier ideas about personal responsibility, showing the consequences of implementing policy without active intention. Again controversially, she portrayed Eichmann not so much as a monster, more as a thoughtless modern creation – hence the banality of evil.

Simone De Beauvoir

(1908–86)

' **One is not born, but rather becomes, woman.** '

The Second Sex (1949)

Born in Paris into a middle-class family, Simone de Beauvoir studied philosophy at the Sorbonne and in 1929 narrowly missed out on first place in the prestigious *agrégation* exam, beaten by Jean-Paul Sartre, with whom she started a relationship – both personal and professional – that was to last a lifetime. She taught philosophy from 1931 to 1943, then embarked on a full-time writing career.

During the 1940s de Beauvoir developed her ideas around an existentialist philosophy that focused on the importance of personal experience in a meaningless world without absolute moral laws, where individuals create their own values and so are responsible for their actions, as they affect both themselves and others. In *The Second Sex* (1949), she focuses on male oppression of women, which she sees as the consequence of a system that assumes male to be the default setting, equating female with 'other'. Identifying a distinction between biological sex and the social and historical construction of gender, de Beauvoir argues that women are as capable of choice as men, they just need to choose to be free.

In her work – novels, essays, autobiography, articles and more – and her personal life, de Beauvoir combined intellectual and philosophical standpoints with political action, embodying the idea that love doesn't automatically mean abandoning freedom or professional success. *The Second Sex* became a bible for subsequent generations of feminists.

Simone Weil

(1909–43)

'Human beings are so made that the ones who do the crushing feel nothing; it is the person crushed who feels what is happening. Unless one has placed oneself on the side of the oppressed, to feel with them, one cannot understand.'

Lectures on Philosophy (1959)

Born in Paris into a secular Jewish family, Simone Weil had a thorough grounding in philosophy by the time she left school and, in 1928, entered the École Normale Supérieure. She saw philosophy as a way to tackle oppression in society and taught manual workers, arguing and writing on their behalf. Deeply influenced by Karl Marx, she saw philosophy as both action and practice.

In 1935 Weil worked in factories as an unskilled female labourer. She found the experience utterly dehumanizing, and was surprised to feel not revolutionary fervour but humiliation and resignation. Ideas about what it meant to be free and to be good took on new significance. Around this time she began to have mystical religious experiences and embraced Christianity. However, during the Second World War the family's Jewish origins put them in danger and they left France for America in 1942. Weil then moved to London to work with the French Resistance. Barely eating and suffering from TB, she effectively wasted away.

Weil's writings remained unpublished until after her death. They include *Gravity and Grace* (1947), a collection of spiritual and philosophical guidelines, *Oppression and Liberty* (1955), political and social papers on war, factory work and language, and *Lectures on Philosophy* (1959). For Weil, life and philosophical reflection were linked at a deep ethical level, and religion articulated the two, with concepts like 'God' and 'soul' up there with 'truth' and 'reality'.

Isaiah Berlin

(1909–97)

'Everything is what it is: liberty is liberty, not equality or fairness or justice or human happiness or a quiet conscience.'

'Two Concepts of Liberty' (1959)

Born in Riga, Latvia, Isaiah Berlin emigrated to Britain with his parents in 1921 to escape anti-Semitism and communism. He studied at Oxford and taught philosophy there in the 1930s, a key contributor to the development of what became known as 'Oxford' or 'ordinary language' philosophy – the belief that many philosophical problems were problems largely because the language used to discuss them had become divorced from everyday meanings. From the early 1940s he was increasingly interested in the history of ideas, and in social and political theory.

Berlin brought these different concerns together in 'Two Concepts of Liberty', his 1958 inaugural lecture as Chichele Professor of Social and Political Theory at Oxford. In considering this seemingly straightforward ideal, he distinguished between negative and positive liberty, the former referring to freedom from external constraints ('I am slave to no man' because society is so structured as to provide the best for me) and the latter to an individual's freedom to follow their own will ('I am my own master' because I can do exactly as I please, regardless of anyone else). These two contradictory interpretations have serious real-life implications at both ends of the political spectrum.

Berlin argued for a nuanced understanding of terminology where what is initially seen as a single concept can in fact cover a number of meanings. A firm pluralist, he believed that life demands constant compromise between often incompatible values.

A. J. Ayer

(1910–89)

'The criterion which
we use to test the
genuineness of apparent
statements of fact is the
criterion of verifiability.'

Language, Truth and Logic (1936)

Born in London, Alfred Jules Ayer was educated at Eton and Christ Church, Oxford, where he was a pupil of the philosopher Gilbert Ryle. After graduating, he went to study at the University of Vienna and there he attended meetings of the Vienna Circle, a group of academics with a background in science and philosophy known as logical positivists who considered mathematical-style logic and clarity of language the only way to proceed when dealing with philosophical – or any other – questions.

Ayer enthusiastically embraced this approach and once he had returned to Oxford he started work on a book that would bring logical positivism to the English-speaking world. Published when he was just twenty-six years old, *Language, Truth and Logic* (1936) introduced the verification principle: only propositions that can be verified through logical analysis or empirically through observation are meaningful (as in literally mean something). This neatly disposes of troublesome areas of debate such as ethics and religion because saying, for example, that it is wrong to steal or that God exists cannot be verified and is therefore meaningless.

Throughout Ayer's long career, he remained convinced that most of the problems that had exercised philosophers over the years were at heart problems of language, with a philosopher's real job being to elucidate the basic concepts of science rather than waste time on metaphysical speculation.

Seongcheol

(1912–93)

'Form *is* formlessness and formlessness *is* form. Not only in words, not only in the realm of philosophy, but in truth, in nature, measurable by scientific methods. This is the Middle Way!'

Seongcheol is the dharma name of Yi Yeongju, who is credited with reforming and revitalizing Korean Buddhism after the Japanese occupation of his country during the Second World War. A bright child who devoured books, he is said to have read the classic novels of Chinese literature by the age of ten and to have traded a sack of rice for a copy of Immanuel Kant's *Critique of Pure Reason*. His interests, then, included Western philosophy, and also science and religion, but it was only when he read *Song of Enlightenment*, a Seon (Zen) text, that he knew he had found the true path.

From the 1950s Seongcheol spearheaded a return to celibacy, strict practice, monasticism and mendicancy for Korean Buddhist monks. Widely recognized as a living Buddha, he challenged the value of 'sudden awakening, gradual cultivation', in which practitioners work through various stages to achieve enlightenment. For Seongcheol, this amounted to the accretion of so much clutter and instead he advocated 'sudden awakening, sudden cultivation', claiming that one's genuine nature could only be realized through ultimate enlightenment.

Seongcheol saw the middle way as being the state of nirvana where all dualities merge, rendering meaningless extremes such as good and bad, self and non-self. He embraced modern science to make his point, citing Einstein's theory of special relativity, which shows that energy and mass, once assumed to be separate, are in fact one and the same.

Alan Turing

(1912–54)

'Can machines think?'

'Computing Machinery and Intelligence',
Mind, Vol. 59 (1950)

Alan Turing graduated in mathematics from Cambridge, completed his PhD at Princeton and became the main player in early work on electronic digital computers and the philosophy of artificial intelligence.

Having formulated the idea of an automatic problem-solving machine while a student, in his 1950 article 'Computing Machinery and Intelligence' Turing proposed a test to determine whether machines can think. This was 'the imitation game'. To start, you need three people: a man, a woman and an interrogator of either sex. In a separate room, asking questions that ignore physical appearance and receiving typed answers, the interrogator has to decide which is male and which female. At some point a machine is substituted for one of them. Can the interrogator distinguish between human and machine? If the answer is no, the machine has passed the Turing Test and so is deemed to be thinking.

During the Second World War Turing had done vital work deciphering German codes at the government's Bletchley Park facility, where the importance of powerful information-handling machines was evident. In 1948 he moved to Manchester University to continue his research into computers and, had the world been a different place, would no doubt have contributed to further developments in the field of artificial intelligence. Instead, charged with a minor homosexual offence, he was subjected to chemical castration and shortly afterwards committed suicide. So much for human intelligence.

Louis Althusser

(1918–90)

'Everything that happens in philosophy has, in the last instance, not only political consequences in theory, but also political consequences in politics: in the political class struggle.'

Essays in Self-Criticism (1974)

Born in Algiers, Louis Althusser studied philosophy at the École Normale Supérieure in Paris, where he then taught for most of his working life, influencing – among others – Michel Foucault and Jacques Derrida. A committed Catholic in his teenage years, he became an equally committed communist after the Second World War, and during the 1960s and 1970s was one of the dominant Marxist philosophers.

In *For Marx* (1965) and *Reading Capital* (1965), Althusser analysed Marxism through the lens of structuralism – the idea that in order to understand the world it is necessary to identify the organizing principles that underpin and determine the interrelationships between its constituent parts. He was looking to formulate a 'theory of theoretical practice', which would allow him to establish a scientific basis for Marxism, as opposed to what he felt to be the current dependence on false ideological concepts that merely described what was happening socio-economically. When left-wing critics who disliked his downgrading of the overtly political challenged his ideas, Althusser published *Essays in Self-Criticism* (1974), in which he redefined his philosophy as the interplay of both theory and politics, describing materialist philosophy as 'class struggle in the field of theory'.

For many, though, Althusser's ideas were becoming increasingly divorced from reality, both intellectually, because people suspected he was just playing with words, and practically, because they believed that at heart Marxism really was a political ideology and not a science.

G. E. M. Anscombe

(1919–2001)

> '**Choosing to kill the innocent as a means to your ends is always murder.**'

'Mr Truman's Degree', pamphlet (1956)

G. E. M. or Elizabeth Anscombe converted to Roman Catholicism as a teenager and religion continued to play an important role throughout her life. She studied at Oxford, but regularly travelled to Cambridge to attend Ludwig Wittgenstein's lectures. Like him, she also became professor of philosophy at Cambridge.

When, in 1956, Oxford University decided to award President Truman an honorary degree, Anscombe objected to celebrating someone who had authorized the bombing of Hiroshima and Nagasaki, killing thousands of civilians. She first published a pamphlet and then wrote at greater length about the nature of intention and moral philosophy. *Intention* (1957) challenges the way philosophers treat knowledge as passive and speculative when in fact intentions have consequences and so carry with them an ethical dimension. In her paper 'Modern Moral Philosophy' (1958) she argued that ideas of what we *ought* to do, with appeals to 'moral duty' and 'right' or 'wrong', are meaningless divorced from an all-powerful Judaeo-Christian lawmaker of a God.

Mary Midgley

(1919–2018)

> ' All moral doctrine, all practical
> suggestions about how we ought
> to live, depend on some belief
> about what human nature is like. '

Beast and Man (1978)

Mary Midgley was educated at Downe House, a progressive
boarding school that had begun life in Charles Darwin's old
home. She won a scholarship to Oxford, where she studied
classics and philosophy. In the 1950s she began to develop
an interest in animal behaviour, reading widely on subjects
including psychology, anthropology and evolutionary theory.

In *Beast and Man: The Roots of Human Nature* (1978)
she defended human nature against what she saw as the
false claims of behaviourism and sociobiology. It seemed
obvious to Midgley that human achievements are based on
abilities and patterns of response shared with other animals,
which means we are not, as the existentialists would have
it, free to create ourselves. As for biological determinism
at the other end of the spectrum – and there were heated
exchanges with Richard Dawkins and his 'selfish gene' on this
issue – Midgley argued that our biological make-up includes
the capacity to develop a shared culture, which in turn
fosters individual creativity.

John Rawls

(1921–2002)

' All social values – liberty and opportunity, income and wealth, and the bases of self-respect – are to be distributed equally unless an unequal distribution of any, or all, of these values is to everyone's advantage. '

A Theory of Justice (1971)

Born and brought up in Baltimore, John Rawls studied and then taught philosophy at Princeton before winning a Fulbright Fellowship to Oxford, where he worked with Isaiah Berlin. On his return to the USA, after teaching at Cornell and MIT, he became professor of philosophy at Harvard in 1962, where he stayed for the next forty years.

In his first major book, *A Theory of Justice* (1971), Rawls sets out to establish the basis of a just society, reconciling the competing demands of freedom and equality. His big idea is 'justice as fairness', which proposes equal basic rights, equal opportunities and active promotion of the interests of the least advantaged. He starts with an experiment that imagines a time before society existed. Working from scratch, how would people order society if they did not know what position they were to hold? To Rawls it seems obvious that they would act to maximize their own chances of well-being – for which read equal access to rights and opportunities. This is not the utilitarian universal greatest-good approach, but rather an appeal to the greatest *average* good.

Rawls identifies two principles here: the liberty principle, which argues that people should have equal claim to basic liberties, and the difference principle, which argues that people with similar talents should have similar life chances and that economic inequalities should bring the greatest benefit to the least advantaged. Without extending basic liberties to those at the lower end of the socio-economic scale, society is not worth living in for anybody.

Thomas Kuhn studied physics at Harvard and then taught science there, gradually becoming more interested in the history of science. He moved to the philosophy department at Berkeley in 1956 to teach history of science and was appointed a full professor in 1961. It was the coming together of these interests that led to the publication in 1962 of *The Structure of Scientific Revolutions*, which cemented his reputation as *the* philosopher of science.

In his book, Kuhn suggests that in any period science, rather than being the slow and steady accumulation of knowledge on the path towards an understanding of physical reality, in fact operates within a set of assumptions – what he calls a scientific paradigm. These assumptions determine the nature of investigations, which depend on existing ideas about what is true. This is 'normal science'. Revolutions take place when, over time, anomalous results pile up and it becomes clear that the current paradigm cannot accommodate the new information.

For Kuhn, ideas from one scientific paradigm are 'incommensurable' with those from another, as they do not share the same conceptual framework. That major upheavals within science take place is undoubted, as shown throughout history – the Copernican revolution is one example cited – and Kuhn expressed the process in evolutionary terms of natural selection. But he saw no rational progression towards the ultimate truth: his was a relativistic world, with scientific truth determined by the consensus of the scientific community.

THomas KuHn

(1922–96)

The resolution of revolutions is selection by conflict within the scientific community of the fittest way to practice future science. The net result of a sequence of such revolutionary selections, separated by periods of normal research, is the wonderfully adapted set of instruments we call modern scientific knowledge.

The Structure of Scientific Revolutions (1962)

Mary Warnock

(1924–2019)

' Without imagination we should be lost; for only with its help can we interpret our experience, turn it into experience of an outer world, and thus make use of it in understanding what and where we are, and what we need to do. '

Imagination and Time (1994)

Mary Warnock studied at Oxford University, where from 1949 to 1966 she taught philosophy, with a particular interest in ethics and existentialism, notably the works of Jean-Paul Sartre. She published accessible books on these subjects and was a regular contributor to BBC radio debates about philosophy.

In *Imagination and Time* (1994), Warnock examines the fundamental role of the imagination in understanding existence and its relationship with time, personal identity and a commitment to the future. Because it allows an individual to think about things that are not here, including things that no longer exist or do not yet exist, imagination is what connects the ephemeral with the permanent, the particular with the universal, so that human beings can make sense of the world in which they live and formulate plans beyond their immediate concerns.

With her successful academic background to provide the ethical framework and her obvious abilities as a communicator to give voice to disparate opinions, Warnock was the obvious candidate to lead a number of major government inquiries. Her commitment to what she called 'the moral idea of society' underpinned her definition of successful policy and explains how she managed to come up with workable rulings in relation to questions about which people had very strong views.

Frantz Fanon

(1925–61)

'Each generation must
out of relative obscurity
discover its mission,
fulfil it, or betray it.'

The Wretched of the Earth (1961)

Born on Martinique, then a French colony, Frantz Fanon grew up in an assimilated bourgeois family. At school, however, he learned about Négritude, a movement working to resist French colonialism, and this had an enormous influence on his thinking. Having experienced white racism first-hand during the Second World War, when Martinique was occupied by pro-Vichy French soldiers and also on joining de Gaulle's Free French forces, he was left in little doubt about France's attitude to its black population.

After the war Fanon studied medicine at Lyon University, specializing in psychiatry. While there he began to write *Black Skin, White Masks* (1952), using his psychiatric training, together with his interest in existentialism and phenomenology, to analyse the intellectual and cultural alienation black people felt in a world dominated by white people and white values. By 1953 he was working at the psychiatric hospital in Blida, Algeria – another French colony, now engaged in a brutal independence struggle. In his last book, *The Wretched of the Earth* (1961), Fanon diagnosed violence as the defining characteristic of colonialism and also the cure. It was only through violence that colonized people could free themselves from oppression and acquire what he called an 'authentic existence'.

Fanon believed that his generation had the chance to bring about decolonialization and when he died – from leukaemia at just thirty-six – national liberation struggles, social revolutions and anti-imperialist movements were vital forces in a world that seemed ready for change.

Born in Poitiers, Michel Foucault was educated in Paris at the École Normale Supérieure and the Sorbonne, where he studied philosophy and psychology. He worked in Sweden, Poland and Germany before returning to France to teach philosophy at the University of Clermont-Ferrand and then at Vincennes, a new experimental university. In 1970 he was appointed professor of the history of systems of thought at the Collège de France in Paris, bringing together his interests in philosophy, psychology, history and linguistics.

Foucault challenged the idea that history can reveal objective truths or teach universal lessons. For him, the knowledge available at a particular period is determined by that period's social norms, its ways of communicating, its cultural expressions and its philosophies. He therefore felt it was necessary to explore the interconnected aspects of culture that give each period its unspoken rules and characteristics, and highlighted the role played here by the exclusion of certain groups of people – particularly those labelled mad, criminal or sexually deviant. He saw power at work everywhere, not merely as something exercised at a certain time by an individual or a class, but as a vast network in which everyone is trapped. This, then, is what creates the 'regime of truth' that underpins a society.

Foucault developed this idea in a range of books throughout his career – the quote here is taken from the first of his three-volume *History of Sexuality* (1976–84).

MicHeL FoucauLt

(1926–84)

'Truth is not by nature
free – nor error servile
– its production is
thoroughly imbued with
relations of power.'

The Will to Knowledge (1976)

Noam Chomsky

(1928–)

'Colorless green ideas
sleep furiously.'

Syntactic Structures (1957)

Noam Chomsky studied linguistics and philosophy at the University of Pennsylvania and spent time researching at Harvard before completing his PhD in linguistics in 1955. He started teaching at MIT that year and, even though he formally retired in 2002, he is still working there.

Chomsky's research at Harvard in the early 1950s informed his groundbreaking books *Syntactic Structures* (1957) and *Aspects of the Theory of Syntax* (1965), which had far-reaching implications for linguistics and also for philosophy. They challenged the prevailing view that children acquired language through training and experience – or, in philosophical terms, empirically. For Chomsky, the speed with which language was mastered suggested an innate predisposition – we are hard-wired. He identified two levels of linguistic knowledge: 'surface structures', or the words used in a particular language, and 'deep structures', or the universal grammar all languages share. When children hear adults speaking, they infer grammatical rules that allow them to construct new sentences, but 'grammatical' is not the same as 'meaningful'. The sentence quoted here illustrates Chomsky's point: it is grammatically accurate nonsense; but no more nonsensical than 'Furiously sleep ideas green colorless', which no one would suggest is grammatical.

Chomsky's work transformed linguistics, but Chomsky has always been just as keen on transforming the world. From the earliest days of his opposition to the Vietnam War, he has been a leading critic of US foreign policy and he continues to influence anti-capitalist campaigners.

Jacques Derrida

(1930–2004)

'There is nothing outside the text ...'

Of Grammatology (1967)

Jacques Derrida was born into a Jewish family in Algeria, which was a French colony at the time. To complicate matters of identity further, in 1940 the Vichy government in France stripped Algerian Jews of their citizenship and Derrida was barred from attending school. Eventually, once the Second World War ended, he went to study in Paris, where he then taught philosophy at the Sorbonne and, for twenty years, philosophy and literature at the École Normale Supérieure. Those two subjects underpinned the approach for which he is best known: deconstruction.

Not so much a theory as a critical method, deconstruction is applicable to any text whatever the subject matter. Instead of expecting a text to have a fixed, universal meaning, representing objective truth, or the author's intentions, the idea is to examine it closely to uncover connections with other texts in different contexts. For Derrida, language is incapable of providing a firm basis for meaning or truth because it actually limits understanding; as he famously said in *Of Grammatology* (1967), the text is all.

As an example of how language limits understanding, Derrida cited the traditional binary oppositions of Western philosophy, arguing that privileging, say, the mind over the body or the rational over the emotional makes one seem better than the other, whereas both are needed for either to have any significance.

Luce Irigaray has made it clear that she does not consider biographical details relevant to any interpretation of her ideas – women have had to fight hard enough to be heard in intellectual circles without unnecessary distractions. In brief, though, she was born in Belgium and in the 1960s went to France, where she was awarded doctorates in philosophy and in linguistics, and also studied psychoanalysis with the analyst Jacques Lacan. With her breakthrough and break-away book, *Speculum of the Other Woman* (1974), she distanced herself from Lacan and what she saw as his exclusively male thought patterns, focusing on the exclusion of women from both philosophy and psychoanalytic theory through the very language used.

For Irigaray, each age is defined by a philosophical issue that is crying out to be examined and, in the 1980s, that issue was sexual difference. In *An Ethics of Sexual Difference* (1984), she looks into how this sexual difference is constructed, concluding that across all areas of life, in language and in debate, the theoretically neutral subject, the ego, in fact reflects only the interests and perspectives of men, while women are sidelined as the non-subject or 'other' – there just to mirror back male concerns.

To prepare the way for a new culture able to accommodate both sexes fairly, Irigaray has worked towards drawing out a specifically feminine language to challenge the existing limits of speech and representation, because, as the title of her 2002 essay collection has it, 'to speak is never neutral'.

Luce Irigaray
(c.1930–)

'Sexual difference is probably the issue in our time which could be our "salvation" if we thought it through.'

An Ethics of Sexual Difference (1984)

RicHarD RorTy

(1931–2007)

'Philosophy makes progress
not by becoming more
rigorous but by becoming
more imaginative.'

Introduction to *Truth and Progress:
Philosophical Papers*, Vol. 3 (1998)

Richard Rorty was born in New York and studied philosophy at the University of Chicago, completing his PhD at Yale. He had a long academic career, as professor of philosophy at Princeton, of humanities at Virginia and of comparative literature at Stanford. This range of interests gave him an impressive overview in his philosophical approach.

In *Philosophy and the Mirror of Nature* (1979), he argued against what he called 'traditional philosophy', by which he meant the search for foundations of knowledge, morality, language and social structure that could be shown to exist above and beyond time and place – outside of history. To his mind this search was meaningless as the results merely gave formal structure to the concerns that were current wherever you happened to be – which he felt explained why, for example, most English-speaking philosophers at the time were linguistic philosophers, while most continental philosophers were phenomenologists.

The answer, for Rorty, was to rethink what philosophy meant. He saw the role of both scientific and philosophical methods as being to contribute 'vocabularies' that people could then adopt, adapt and abandon over time according to their usefulness. By getting rid of outmoded vocabularies that failed to take account of people's place in history, and by treating philosophy as 'a voice in a conversation' rather than an academic subject divorced from its utility, Rorty believed that both philosophy and societies would benefit.

Amartya Sen

(1933–)

'The perspective of human capability focuses ... on the ability ... of people to lead the lives they have reason to value.'

Development as Freedom (1999)

Amartya Sen was born in Santiniketan, West Bengal, and went to university in Kolkata and then Cambridge, studying economics at both. In 1956 he interrupted research for his PhD in Cambridge to return to India and head up the economics department at Kolkata's newly established Jadavpur University. Two years later he was offered a fellowship at Cambridge and returned to study philosophy.

The combination of economics and philosophy made perfect sense as Sen's areas of interest in economics – in particular, social choice theory and an analysis of social injustice and deprivation – draw on logic and ethics, taking him into the wider sphere of political philosophy. This culminated in the early 1980s in the formulation of his capability approach. Rather than the usual focus on increasing GDP, technical progress and industrialization as a way of tackling social and economic problems of inequality, poverty and the associated lack of liberty and rights, Sen favoured a human-scale approach, looking at the effects of economic policies on the well-being of communities. He stressed the importance of fostering conditions in which people could lead the kind of life they would value, which meant improving chances and choices, and in *Development as Freedom* (1999), Sen identified five requirements: political freedoms, economic facilities, social opportunities, transparency guarantees and protective security.

Over his long career, Sen has taught at numerous universities. In 1998 he was awarded the Nobel Prize in Economic Sciences for his contribution to welfare economics.

Born in Daegu, Korea, Jaegwon Kim studied French literature at Seoul National University before moving to the USA to continue his education. He graduated from Dartmouth College, with a degree in French, mathematics and philosophy, and went on to do his PhD in philosophy at Princeton. He spent most of his working life teaching philosophy at Brown University.

Kim was best known for his work on philosophy of mind, particularly the problem of mental causation – whether intentional thoughts or states of mind can result in intentional actions. This was linked not only to the age-old mind–body question but also to supervenience, or the nature of the relationships between sets of attributes or facts. He argued that mental states could not be reduced to physical properties of the brain. His work on supervenience led to a detailed study of causation itself, with all the metaphysical ramifications. How are we to marry acceptance of the laws of physics, which posit a physical explanation for events in the physical world, and the significance of mental states in determining subsequent events?

Kim argued for the need to incorporate human experience and cognition into a naturalistic world-view. In his book *Mind in a Physical World* (1998), he warned against over-reliance on a mechanistic approach and thinking that philosophical problems can be solved simply and easily, without having 'to pay a heavy metaphysical price'.

Jaegwon Kim

(1934–2019)

'There are no free lunches in philosophy any more than in real life, and I believe the cheap ones aren't worth the money. We might as well go for the real stuff and pay the price.'

Mind in a Physical World (1998)

RoBerT NoZick

(1938–2002)

' Moral philosophy sets the
background for, and boundaries of,
political philosophy. What persons
may and may not do to one another
limits what they may do through
the apparatus of a state, or do
to establish such an apparatus. '

Anarchy, State, and Utopia (1974)

Born in New York, Robert Nozick studied at Columbia University, then Princeton and Oxford as a Fulbright Scholar. He taught at Princeton, Harvard and Rockefeller universities, before moving to Harvard permanently in 1969. As well as becoming professor of philosophy there, he was also president of the American Philosophical Association.

Nozick established his reputation with his first book, *Anarchy, State, and Utopia* (1974), in which he puts forward arguments for a minimal state that confines itself to providing security for people and property. This was his riposte to John Rawls's influential *A Theory of Justice* (1971). Where Rawls talked of 'justice as fairness' and saw the need to redistribute wealth to help the least advantaged, Nozick took a different approach with his 'entitlement theory of justice'. According to Nozick, individuals are just that – their own people: they do not serve anyone else's ends; they own their bodies, their abilities and the fruits of those abilities. No one has the right to take by force what results from someone else's labour, and that 'no one' includes the state, so there's no place for redistribution for the greater good here.

The idea of a minimal state that deals only with problems of 'force, theft and fraud' will guard against any propensity towards anarchy that might arise from libertarianism. But this is no social contract of the old sort: in Nozick's system individuals' rights precede any contract with the state. Far from being restrictive, the minimal state is, for Nozick, a 'framework for utopia', allowing people to achieve different goals depending on their particular talents.

Angela Davis

(1944–)

'**Radical simply means "grasping things at the root".**'

'Let Us All Rise Up Together', lecture
given at Spelman College, Atlanta, 1987

Angela Davis was born in Birmingham, Alabama, at a time when African Americans were denied basic civil rights. As a child, she was told by her mother how segregation worked but encouraged to believe that she could help promote change. Davis won a scholarship to Brandeis University, Massachusetts, and while there met the philosopher Herbert Marcuse, who – she said years later – showed her it was possible to be an academic and an activist, a scholar and a revolutionary. Her career path was set.

After completing her studies in Europe, Davis was appointed assistant philosophy professor at UCLA in 1969, but a year later she was dismissed for being a Communist Party member. She became involved in the campaign to free the Soledad Brothers, imprisoned black activists, but when four people were shot dead, it turned out that the guns used were registered in Davis's name. Suddenly she was on the FBI's 'Ten Most Wanted' list, charged with conspiracy, kidnap and murder. She was in prison for sixteen months before being tried and acquitted on all charges in 1972.

These experiences led her to identify and campaign against what she called the 'prison-industrial complex', a modern form of slavery with the black population disproportionately represented. By now widely seen as a political radical, Davis resumed her involvement in various protest groups while pursuing her academic career. She played a major role organizing student demonstrations and arguing for civil, women's and prisoners' rights. She still continues to write and lecture, a vocal advocate for active resistance in the face of oppression.

Peter Singer was born in Melbourne and studied law, history and philosophy at university there before deciding to focus on philosophy. He did postgraduate work at Oxford and then lectured there for three years before moving to academic posts in New York and Melbourne. In 1999 he was appointed professor of bioethics at Princeton.

One of Singer's earliest works, *Animal Liberation* (1975), looks at the heartless way humans treat animals and is often credited with starting the animal rights movement. In *Practical Ethics* (1979), he broadened the range of topics covered to include, among other things, the taking of life as it relates to humans (including abortion and euthanasia) and animals; extremes of wealth and poverty between people and between nations; civil disobedience, terrorism and violence; and, in the 2011 edition, climate change.

In these and subsequent books, Singer's concern is to guide practical responses to real-world problems based on sound ethical analysis. Following the utilitarian line, he argues that the highest moral good is the greatest happiness – and the least pain – for the greatest number, while respecting individual autonomy. The guiding principle is effective altruism, using evidence and reasoning to determine the best way to benefit others, wherever they are in the world and whoever or whatever they are.

Peter Singer

(1946–)

'An ethical judgment that is no good in practice must suffer from a theoretical defect as well, for the whole point of ethical judgments is to guide practice.'

Practical Ethics (3rd edition, 2011)

Martha Nussbaum

(1947–)

'Philosophy should not
be written in detachment
from real life.'

Cultivating Humanity (1997)

Martha Nussbaum was born in New York and taught philosophy and classics at Harvard, Brown and Oxford universities before being appointed professor of law and ethics at the University of Chicago. She has written on a wide range of subjects, including Greek and Roman philosophy, gender equality, international development, political theory and policy, and education.

In *Cultivating Humanity* (1997), Nussbaum argues for liberal education to create a new generation of thinkers who will transcend differences of class, gender and nationality in order to tackle global concerns. Drawing on Socrates and the Stoics, she highlights the importance of critical self-examination and aspirations to be citizens of the world. A champion of multiculturalism, she defends subject areas such as minority and gay studies, emphasizing their contribution to critical reasoning and world citizenship, and stresses the value of literature for furthering narrative imagination as applied to ethical questions.

Academic theory has taken practical turns throughout Nussbaum's career. From 1986 to 1993 she advised the United Nations University World Institute for Development Economics Research, which promotes peace and progress by bringing together leading scholars to address international problems. In 2004 she was a founding president of the Human Development and Capability Association, which fosters global well-being through research in economics, health, education, law and government.

Cornel West

(1953–)

'Being a hope is being in motion, on the move with body on the line, mind set on freedom, soul full of courage, and heart shot through with love. Being a hope is forging moral and spiritual fortitude, putting on intellectual armor, and being willing to live and die for the empowerment of the wretched of the earth.'

'Race Matters in Twenty-First-Century America', new introduction to *Race Matters* (2018)

Cornel West was born in Tulsa, Oklahoma, and brought up in Sacramento, California, where he was deeply influenced by his Baptist church and the Black Panther Party, whose offices were nearby. In church he heard moving testimonies from other African Americans about their struggles, both current and historic, while from the Panthers, who introduced him to the works of Karl Marx, he learned the importance of political activism. An undergraduate at Harvard and a postgraduate at Princeton, with a PhD in philosophy, he went on to teach philosophy, religion and African American studies at Yale, Harvard, Princeton and Union Theological Seminary. He is currently professor of the practice of public philosophy at Harvard.

Race Matters (1993) is a collection of essays that explore the centrality of racism in American history. Initially published a year after the acquittal of the police officers who attacked Rodney King, sparking riots in Los Angeles, it covers a range of issues, including the crisis in black leadership, myths surrounding black sexuality and the new black conservatism. The quote here is taken from the twenty-fifth-anniversary edition of the book, which remains frighteningly relevant today.

West's work is wide-ranging. His books analyse issues of race, class and justice within a philosophical framework and he has always been a political activist as well as an academic, participating in demonstrations and involving himself with causes that he feels are just.

Born in Minneapolis, Michael Sandel studied politics at Brandeis University. He then went to Oxford as a Rhodes Scholar and undertook postgraduate research in philosophy. In 1980 he began teaching political philosophy at Harvard. Apart from a short period as a visiting professor at the Sorbonne in 2001, he has remained at Harvard, where he is now professor of government. His influence extends beyond the university world, as he is well known for hosting regular radio and television debates that explore the philosophical ideas behind issues of current concern, earning him the title 'the public philosopher'.

From the start, Sandel questioned the prevailing philosophical approach taken in *A Theory of Justice* by John Rawls, asking whether it makes sense to look for principles of justice and individual rights that remain fixed regardless of different ideas about what actually constitutes virtue and the good life. While Rawls's utilitarian talk of the greater good might sound admirable, it ignored such areas as political and moral rights, which protect individual freedoms of belief and bind people to their communities.

In *Justice: What's the Right Thing to Do?* (2009), Sandel asks what we really mean when we talk about justice. If a just society is one that distributes income and wealth fairly, balances rights and duties, provides opportunities and rewards service, who is empowered to decide what each person is due? In his books and in his public appearances, Sandel shows that while there are no simple answers, it is important to keep the conversation going.

MicHaeL SanDeL

(1953–)

'The way things are does not determine the way they ought to be.'

Justice (2009)

Kwame Anthony Appiah

(1954–)

'People often recommend relativism because they think it will lead to tolerance. But if we cannot learn from one another what it is right to think and feel and do, then conversation between us will be pointless.'

Cosmopolitanism (2006)

Kwame Anthony Appiah was born in London. When he was a baby, the family moved to Ghana, but as a teenager he went to school in England and then studied philosophy at Cambridge. He has taught at universities in Ghana and America, including Yale, Harvard and Princeton, and is currently professor of philosophy and law at New York University.

With increasing globalization, and the changes to existing ways of life this entails, Appiah is interested in philosophical issues around race and identity, together with moral theory. From an ethical standpoint, we accept that everyone is entitled to certain basic resources to allow them to live in a dignified fashion, but our own identities and concerns often blind us to inequalities elsewhere. As citizens of the world, should we be looking for an absolute moral code or accept that everyone has their own values?

For Appiah, there is a middle way. In *Cosmopolitanism: Ethics in a World of Strangers* (2006), he argues that we have global obligations where universal standards are concerned but should also preserve local values and communities. Only by actively celebrating our different practices and beliefs, becoming better informed about them through dialogue, will we find a way to mutually flourish.

Simon Critchley

(1960–)

'You'll Never Walk Alone'

from the Rodgers and Hammerstein
musical *Carousel* (1945)

Simon Critchley left school at sixteen with no intention of pursuing an academic career – he was more interested in punk rock. However, in 1982 he went to study philosophy and literature at the University of Essex. His PhD thesis became his first book, *The Ethics of Deconstruction: Derrida and Levinas* (1992). He is now professor of philosophy at the New School for Social Research in New York, where his interests include continental philosophy, psychoanalysis, ethics and political theory.

Critchley has published widely, with books on all these subjects and more. His *Very Little... Almost Nothing* (1997) discusses religious disappointment, while *Infinitely Demanding* (2007) tackles political disappointment, and the ramifications of both these setbacks. And then there's *What We Think About When We Think About Football* (2017). More than once Critchley has said, 'My only religious commitment is to Liverpool Football Club.' Since this book starts with Laozi's thousand-mile journey, it seems fitting to end secure in the knowledge that – as the fans sing on the terraces at Anfield – we are not walking alone.

Index of Philosophers